IDENTIFIED

IDENTIFIED

Knowing Who You Are in Christ
& Moving Forward in Your Purpose

COURTNAYE RICHARD

Christian Women's Blogger of Inside Out with Courtnaye

WESTBOW
PRESS®
A DIVISION OF THOMAS NELSON
& ZONDERVAN

WestBow Press books may be ordered through booksellers or by contacting:

WestBow Press
A Division of Thomas Nelson & Zondervan
1663 Liberty Drive
Bloomington, IN 47403
www.westbowpress.com
1 (866) 928-1240

Interior Graphics: Fabio Formaggio

ISBN: 978-1-5127-5287-8 (sc)
ISBN: 978-1-5127-5288-5 (hc)
ISBN: 978-1-5127-5286-1 (e)

Library of Congress Control Number: 2016912921

Print information available on the last page.

WestBow Press rev. date: 8/19/2016

This book is dedicated to the women who have been created for such a time as this.

~ESTHER 4:14

ACKNOWLEDGEMENTS

First and foremost, I really would like to take this precious time to thank my Heavenly Father!!! God, You are so AMAZING! I don't have enough tongues to praise You! I am in total awe of You and who You are! I could not have done any of this without You! Thank You so much for Your supernatural guidance through your precious Holy Spirit, grace, favor, and for the love and sacrifice of Your Son and my Lord and Savior, Jesus Christ! I am forever grateful to You for all You have done in my life and through these pages. Thank You for trusting me with your Holy Word and the gift to write. I love You so much!

My deepest appreciation to my husband, Calvin "Go Hard" Richard. You have been so awesome throughout this entire writing process! Thank you so much for your amazing unconditional love, support, encouragement, wisdom, listening ear, and for the hand massage! I'll never forget you telling me, "Now, go write!" Also, thank you for helping hold down the fort at home with our three beautiful children, Armond, Cali, and Chase. I am so very grateful to my kids for being patient with me as I spent many hours grinding on this project. You guys willingly sacrificed your mom for a few months in order to help many women across this globe to draw closer to God, know who they are in Christ, and move forward in their purposes. I love you all and I *will* keep my word and take you guys for a weekend getaway and to Six Flags!

I would also like to thank my mom who started my writing career off! Thanks mom for all the bookstore trips when I was young and for buying my first of many journals and notebooks. I love you greatly! Even though my dad is no longer here on earth, he was a great encourager for anything I put my hands to do. I really do miss him. I would also like say a *big* thank you to my baby sister, Candyce Thompson! Girl, you know you were here for me during this process! I can't thank you enough for your listening ear, wisdom, super encouragement, and simply being there whenever I needed to talk or needed prayer. Thank you so much, sis! I would like to say that I love my big sister, Chauntelle Randle! Girl, no matter how many miles apart we are, distance could never change the love that I have for you. Thanks for always being my sweet, loving, big sister!

I would also like to say a *huge* thank you to my very good friend Marilyn Powell from college and DM Powered! Hey *life coach*, because that's exactly what you were for me during this process! I love the fact that you were there for me at the drop of a dime when I needed prayer. All I had to do was get on Facebook and inbox you and say, "Girl, pray for me," or "I need motivation!" You were right there interceding for me and for the success of this book. Girl, thank you *big time*!

I would also like to say thank you to Pastor Willie Monnet, Sr. and Minister Claudette Monnet of Smoking for Jesus Ministry. You both truly helped me to grow in my walk with the Lord and I am forever grateful for your help in my spiritual journey. I have to say a great *big* thank you to my mentor and really good friend Minister Tara Griffin! Other than God and my husband, you just *know* me! There's nothing hidden in our relationship. I'm an open book with you, and I thank God for you and your husband, Minister Gayln Griffin's love, late night counseling, mentorship, prayers, fellowship, encouragement, and long conversations through the years. I love you both and your children so very much! I also want to shout a really big thank you to Pastor Ross Chandler and his beautiful wife Meaghen Chandler of First Baptist Church of Marble Falls for welcoming me and my family with open and loving arms. Pastor Ross, I can't express how much your willingness to help me with this project and your servant heart have been a tremendous blessing to me! Keep showing the world Jesus Christ through your actions. You're shining bright!

I also want to say thanks to my father-in-law, Calvin, Sr., for your great wisdom and for you and Charmaine watching the kiddos for us! And thanks so much to my in-laws Madlyn & Michael Bagneris for your love and support of me and this project. God opened the door for me. Yay! I love you guys! Also, thanks to my Uncle T for teaching me that the word of God is taught line upon line and precept upon precept, and for those priceless biblical nuggets of advice when I come home to visit. They really are golden! And thank you Uncle Laird for your awesome godly wisdom right when I needed it most! Keep sharing the Good News through traveling wherever the Lord leads you and through your musical gift. Thanks to my praying, phenomenal, patient, editor Nicole Grant of Ardeo Lit! Wow! You rocked it! I can't thank you enough for pressing through all of the deadlines, long hours, encouragement, and pushing me through email saying, "Keep writing!" I loved it! That was truly, truly awesome and very commendable. I would recommend you to anyone, any day, and I will! And I certainly cannot forget Rachel Biagini of Biagini Photography for her phenomenal photos! You stepped in right when I needed you most in this process. You are truly an amazing woman and photographer, and I thank God for you!

I also would like to thank WestBow Press for your hard work, dedication, and professionalism in getting this manuscript printed and published. To all of my friends, family, and church family who encouraged, supported, and prayed for me, I love you and thank you so much!

CONTENTS

INTRODUCTION

"It is God who enables us, along with you, to stand firm for Christ. He has commissioned us, and he has identified us as his own by placing the Holy Spirit in our hearts as the first installment that guarantees everything he has promised us."
—2 CORINTHIANS 1:21–22

We are living in a time when we have to stand strong for Christ *together*. God is calling you and me to be agents of change, beacons of light, and bold witnesses to the life of faith. But it starts with us *truly* knowing who we are in Christ.

Listen. Once you have confessed that you are a sinner, repented of your sins, established the belief in your heart that God sent His only begotten Son Jesus Christ to die on a cross for your sins, and have accepted Him as your Lord and Savior, then you are saved. You are **IDENTIFIED** in Christ. The next step is moving forward, growing in your faith, and doing what He has called you to do!

Jesus Christ is coming back soon. The state of the world and the church is a prophetic sign of this truth. Jesus said in Luke 19:13, "Occupy until I come." Meaning use the gifts and talents that He has given you, and through the power of the Holy Spirit—move!

The Bible tells us in 2 Peter 1:21, "For the prophecy came not in old times by the will of man: but holy men of God spake as they were moved by the Holy Spirit" (KJV). Do you want to do the will of God? Do you want to walk out your God-given potential? Has the Lord given you a vision to do something awesome for His glory? If so, then what's holding you back?

It's high time to move as the Holy Spirit leads you to do what God is calling you to do, my sister. This is not the time to lose sight of who you are in Christ. Too many people are losing ground in their identity and beginning to lose faith—and our great enemy Satan loves it!

He is strategically stealing people's identity and causing thousands to doubt their God-given abilities within them. But don't let him do it to you! Fight with everything inside of you to protect your identity and believe by faith that God can and will do great things through you. The Bible reassures us of this when it says in Matthew 19:26, "With God all things are possible."

It is not by chance that you either heard of this book or decided to pick it up. God is commissioning you right now to walk in the power of the Holy Spirit and win souls for His Kingdom. He has placed gifts inside of you, called you before you were formed in your mother's womb, and predestined you to be a prophetic voice to the nations.

Whether through a major platform, in your local church, in your community, through social media, or beyond—*you* were created for such a time as this. God wants to use *you*.

So don't lose your self-worth in what others think of you. Don't be intimidated. Don't compare yourself to others. Don't doubt what God can do in and through you in these last days. And *don't* allow the enemy to stagnate your progress with fear and doubt. Instead, believe what God says about you and believe who you are in Christ. Because as an IDENTIFIED woman in Christ:

You are a royal priesthood.

You are His masterpiece.

You are child of God.

You are called to have life and have life more abundantly.

You were created for a purpose.

You are **IDENTIFIED**!

It's time to *know* who you are in Christ and move forward in faith. Are you ready to make your thumbprint in the world? If so, let's move on…

PART ONE:

Knowing Who You Are in Christ

"And now you Gentiles have also heard the truth, the Good News that God saves you. And when you believed in Christ, he identified you as his own by giving you the Holy Spirit, whom he promised long ago."
—EPHESIANS 1:13 (NLT)

CHAPTER 1

Spiritual Thumbprint: The Stamp of an IDENTIFIED Woman

"And when you believed in Christ, He identified you as His own by giving you the Holy Spirit, whom He promised long ago."
—EPHESIANS 1:13

You have been called for such a time as this! But before you set out to turn the world upside down, we need to talk about some basic, yet important fundamentals. It's crucial that you really *know* who you are in Christ. Because if you don't know, later on as you prepare for, anticipate, and walk out your calling, the enemy will raise up an army to try to steal that knowledge from you. So let's start here!

Once you accept Jesus Christ as your Lord and Savior, know that you are an IDENTIFIED woman. The Holy Spirit lives inside of you. Own your inheritance! The reason why I'm telling you this is because in this life, our great enemy Satan will try to shake your foundation. Remember, he's a thief. So knowing who you are in Christ now, will give you some fighting power later.

Why is knowing your identity upfront so important? Simply because once you know who you are in Christ, when you embrace the power that is within you, it will be much easier for you to make a spiritual thumbprint in this dark world. God wants you to shine bright, so that others will want what you have, which is Jesus. Others also need to know who they are in Him, and that's where you come into the picture.

There's only one you. No one else has your thumbprint. From a natural perspective, this is the way you are IDENTIFIED. But once you have accepted your *new* identity in Christ, you've been reborn. In spiritual terms, you've been born again. In 2 Corinthians 5:17 the Bible explains, "This means that anyone who belongs to Christ has become a new person. The old life is gone; a new life has begun!" So you have a new spiritual thumbprint. And Jesus is calling you, dear sister, to make your mark in this world for Him.

YOU ARE ADOPTED INTO THE FAITH

It all starts here! I thank God for the Apostle Paul's conversion and his obedience to answer the call in helping the Gentiles receive the free gift of salvation. It was God's plan to adopt us from the beginning of time! Ephesians 1:1 and 5 assures us of this fact saying, "This letter is from Paul, chosen by the will of God to be an apostle of Christ Jesus—God decided in advance to adopt us into His own family by bringing us to Himself through Jesus Christ. This is what He wanted to do, and it gave Him great pleasure."

It gave God great pleasure to adopt us into His family. What a blessing! What an inheritance! So let's do what Ephesians 1:6 tells us, "So we praise God for the glorious grace he has poured out on us who belong to his dear Son." Go on! Give Him a shout of praise right in the middle of this reading. Smile, laugh out loud, and rejoice! You have been adopted, sis. And so have I! We are in very good hands.

Let's look at this spiritual reality in the natural sense for a moment. Imagine two parents who already have biological children, yet they have a desire to adopt another child into their family. In this case, they go through the adoption process and then one day, everything goes through! These parents accept this new child as their own, and train him or her up with unconditional love and discipline. Well, that's how it is when you and I have been adopted into God's family. You see, the Jews were God's very own special people, and they still are. Yet, the Gentiles had to be adopted into the family of God through Christ Jesus. That's where the Apostle Paul comes into play. He was the one chosen to preach not only to the Jews, but also to the Gentiles. Most of us are Gentiles. So thank God for Jesus, and thank God for Paul!

I need to pause here for a moment to speak to the woman reading this book that has been adopted in the natural sense. I hope that you had a good experience. I hope that your adoptive family members were kind and loving people. However, if your adoptive journey was less than ideal, then I pray that God heals your heart. And I pray that you have or will receive *His* adoption. But no matter who you are reading this, I want to encourage you with these words, God loves you. He says in His word, "I will never fail you. I will never abandon you" (Hebrews 13:5). Once you have been IDENTIFIED in Christ, He claims you as His own. He will never abuse you. And He promises that He will never leave you or forsake you. He will take care of you.

So walk in this God-given confidence, no matter who you are. And hold onto the word found in Galatians 3:26–29 that tells us, "For you are all children of God through faith in Christ Jesus. And all who have been united with Christ in baptism have put on Christ, like putting on new clothes. There is no longer Jew or Gentile, slave or free, male or female. For you are all one in Christ Jesus. And now that you belong to Christ, you are the true children of Abraham. You are his heirs, and God's promise to Abraham belongs to you." According to God's word, you are IDENTIFIED as His child.

YOU ARE VALUABLE

Now that you are grounded in the fact that you are adopted, know that you are valuable to God. Know that He wants to use you in these last days. He has chosen you to be a prophetic voice to the nations to proclaim the Good News. The Lord wants to use *you* to win souls for the Kingdom of Heaven. That's right! He wants to use you in your home, church, workplace, online, and in your community. He wants to use you as you shop in the mall, as you talk to friends and family on the phone, and even as you communicate through email or direct messaging.

You are very important to God. Your voice is very important to Him. And that's what being valuable is mainly about. The word, *value,* is defined as importance, worth, and usefulness. As I stated before, He wants to use you. Think about it in the natural sense, again. In the workplace, or even in a ministry role, a boss or leader would consider you valuable to the company or church because they see your worth, your potential. And of course they would want to use you to help do something awesome for the company, in this case, the Kingdom. It's all because they see something awesome in you! Are you getting this?

That's how God sees you. Once you have been IDENTIFIED in Christ Jesus, you are of great value! He knows that what has been placed inside of you can be used mightily for the advancement of His Kingdom. God wants nothing more than to see an expanding number of people saved. He wants more and more people to know their worth as you do.

So don't let anyone tell you that you're not worth anything or that you're not valuable. Because you are! You are valuable and precious in His sight. Encourage yourself in the word through Psalm 139:17, "How precious are your thoughts about me, O God. They cannot be numbered!" Amen! Jesus loves you and wants nothing but the best for you. His thoughts are precious towards you!

ACCEPT HIS FORGIVENESS

I will tell you one of the greatest hindrances when you are doing what God has called you to do is self-condemnation. Our great enemy Satan has done a pretty good job—unfortunately—of making us feel condemned when we have messed up. He absolutely loves to paralyze us in this manner. Yet, the word of God is right there to free us from this paralysis. When you and I mess up, we have the freedom to go to God to ask His forgiveness, so that He can cleanse us from all unrighteousness. In 1 John 1:9 it says, "If we confess our sins to him, he is faithful and just to forgive us our sins, and to cleanse us from all unrighteousness" (KJV). This is forgiveness in action. We just have to learn how to accept it.

I know from experience what self-condemnation feels like. It's heavy! I remember when I did something that made me think God could not use me again because of my sin. It was a moment where I totally disrespected my husband. I just verbally ripped him apart with my mouth, while putting him down. The flesh girl was full on! I had no self-control in this instance. Of course, I felt horrible when the incident was over, because I knew that Ephesians 5:33 says, "So again I say, each man must love his wife as he loves himself, and the wife must respect her husband."

After beating myself up mentally and apologizing profusely, he accepted my apology and forgave me. But then he started encouraging me from every angle! He reminded *me* not to condemn myself. Wow! I really do have a great *loving* husband. Because no doubt, I'd messed up, that was a given. And yes, I felt really bad for my unrighteous actions. But he was absolutely right. I couldn't stay there and sulk in that reality. Instead, I needed to confess my sin, ask for forgiveness and mercy, repent, and let go of the self-condemnation.

And let me say here, I knew the verses on "no condemnation," yet when I was smack-dab in the middle of my feeling of defeat, it was hard to see that God could forgive me. And that's where the lie from Satan was created. The enemy is the father of lies. He speaks against truth. In the end, the word of God prevailed! And I'm grateful for that. The Lord revealed to me that Peter messed up too. But that Jesus still loved him and used him mightily to turn this world upside down for the Kingdom! The key is having a repentant heart. And I did exactly that! Repented.

It's also important to know that Jesus is our greatest intercessor. The Bible tells us in 1 John 2:1, "My dear children, I am writing this to you so that you will not sin. But if anyone does sin, we have an advocate who pleads our case before the Father. He is Jesus Christ, the one who is truly righteous." This is Good News! Now granted, I need to add here that this doesn't give us license to sin. A mistake is a mistake. Remember, the first sentence says, "I am writing this to you so that you will not sin." So let's trust in the Holy Spirit to lead us to do the right thing and make the right decisions as we walk out our Christian lives. Amen!

Listen, sis, the main point here is that if we are going to make our stamp in this world, then we are going to have to let go of the weight of self-condemnation. Romans 8:1 tells us, "So now there is no condemnation for those who belong to Christ Jesus." This is God's word to us as believers. So *claim* this delivering Scripture. Walk in this freedom, and keep pressing towards the mark of the high calling! Others need you.

BE WHO GOD SAYS YOU ARE

I hope you *know* that you have been adopted into the faith through Christ Jesus, that you are valuable to the Lord, and that you are forgiven. Now you need to be who *God* says you are. You are chosen. You are a royal priesthood. You are a holy nation. You are God's special possession. You have been called out of darkness and into His marvelous light as 1 Peter 2:9 states. And you have been called for a specific purpose.

Now is not the time to be losing ground in who you are or who He has called you to be. If you really want to know your purpose and how to walk in it successfully, then I encourage you to follow what Romans 12:2 says, "Don't copy the behavior and customs of this world, but let God transform you into a new person by changing the way you think. Then you will learn to know God's will for you, which is good and pleasing and perfect." When you begin to let God transform your mind through the power of His word, then His good, pleasing, and perfect will, will begin to unfold for you. And then *live*.

Live like an IDENTIFIED woman in Christ. Let your light shine. Let the Lord lead you in whatever He has called you to do. And trust that He will complete the work that He has begun in you until Christ comes back for you. Philippians 1:6 says, "And I am certain that God, who began the good work within you, will continue his work until it is finally finished on the day when Christ returns." Know who you are and what He says about you, while watching out for the deception of the enemy in these last days. Because too many people are beginning to lose sight of who they are right now.

LET'S TALK ABOUT THE IDENTITY CRISIS

There are a lot of things that can cause you to have an identity crisis. Things such as what I just finished writing about in regards to not knowing who God says you are, low self-esteem, self-condemnation, comparison, your own insecurities, and the list could literally go on and on. By definition, an *identity crisis* is defined as a feeling of unhappiness or confusion that's caused by not being sure of who you really are or what your true purpose is in life. Quite honestly, this can happen to anyone—even the strongest Christian. That's why we have to continually guard our hearts from this cunning deception.

I believe the way to overcome an identity crisis is by standing strong on God's word, praying fervently, speaking positive affirmations over yourself, and confessing your sins. Because if you allow the confusion, alluring thoughts, or depression to defeat or overtake you, then that's when you leave yourself unprotected and open for an enemy invasion. And it slowly develops into an identity crisis. But in order to remedy it, you almost have to stand up and declare who God says you are out loud and believe it at all costs! It's like you're fighting to stand up for your identity. And unfortunately, there are a lot of people across the globe who are weak in the fight right now.

In this chapter, I need to address one particular identity crisis that we're facing in our current world today. The reason why I'm bringing it up is because I believe that you and I play a vital role in it. At the time of this writing, too many people are beginning to lose sight of who they are in our generation. One major crisis that we're challenged with today, even within the body of Christ, is the hot-button topic of homosexuality and same-sex marriage.

I hope you haven't decided to turn to the next chapter to avoid dealing with this crisis of today, because *together* I believe that we can help those who are losing their identity find it again—even if that is *you*. I want to discuss this subject in the context of lesbianism, since I am talking to women specifically in this book. So let's talk for a moment.

As you may have noticed, we've reached a point in our reality where, instead of a woman wanting to be a wife, she is now open to being a husband. Instead of mothers and fathers in a family, we now have two moms wanting to parent, which then brings on an identity crisis for the child or children in this type of environment. In my own experience of our newfound society, as I was shopping in the mall with my kids one Saturday afternoon, I happened to notice two young ladies sitting on a sofa kissing...openly. Because of the new laws passed on gay rights, I didn't feel like I could or should really do anything. My first thought was to shield my kids from seeing them and hurry them along, which I did. But in reality, this is the new way of the land according to this contemporary worldview.

Let me explain something to you. Even though I was initially appalled by what I had just witnessed right in front of me and my kids, when I got into my car, I really felt a tug from the Lord. It was as if He was correcting me and quickening me about my reaction. Instead of being upset about it, He quickened me to pray for them. Instead of being disgusted by it, He placed a newfound burden in my heart to seek Him on how to effectively witness to them through His word with love versus disgust or judgment. There is no doubt in my mind that we are indeed facing an identity crisis, because we are. And deliverance is the antidote. But I also believe that as Christians, we have to learn *how* to deal with it the way Jesus would do it, rather than the way the religious Pharisees and Sadducees did it.

Now, I know that I won't be popular for writing about this issue, but if talking about it is going to help set some women free today, while also putting a fresh new charge in us as believers to *help* those facing the crisis in God's way, then I'm up for the challenge. Are you? Remember, Abraham prayed for the people in Sodom and Gomorrah before God brought about His final judgment upon them. And most of us know that the only way Lot was able to escape with his family was because of his righteousness, with the exception of his wife who turned back and was turned into a pillar of salt (read Genesis 18:16–33).

But the point here is that Abraham prayed. And we also know, according to Scripture, that God heard Abraham's prayer. But even though the prayer was heard, God was looking for righteousness in the others. And He did not find it, so He moved. I believe that's where we are again today as it relates to this identity crisis. God is looking for righteousness, *before* He moves again.

Trust me. I know this is a tough one. But we have to face it. And repentance is necessary. The reality is that God destroyed cities like Sodom and Gomorrah over sexual immorality. The Bible tells us that they were for our example, a warning for our world and our time. In 2 Peter 2:6 it says, "Later, God condemned the cities of Sodom and Gomorrah and turned them into heaps of ashes. He made them an example of what will happen to ungodly people." Again, this is a call for prayer and repentance. Just like He gave Noah and Lot time to get their families out before judgment, He is warning us again today.

So no matter who is reading this book at this time, know that before He judges, change is always a choice. And this goes for any area. Let the truth of God's word transform your life. Take note of what 1 Corinthians 6:9–11 states, "Don't you realize that those who do wrong will not inherit the Kingdom of God? Don't fool yourselves. Those who indulge in sexual sin, or who worship idols, or commit adultery, or are male prostitutes, or practice homosexuality, or are thieves, or greedy people, or drunkards, or are abusive, or cheat people—none of these will inherit the Kingdom of God." This is the New Testament. This is God's uncompromising word.

But look at the hope in it for someone who is truly IDENTIFIED in Christ. Look at the change that has taken place. In 1 Corinthians 6:12 it states, "Some of you were once like that. But you were cleansed; you were made holy; you were made right with God by calling on the name of the Lord Jesus Christ and by the Spirit of our God." Do you see the difference?

As an IDENTIFIED woman in Christ, there will be change that is evident in your life. So let God's righteousness shine through you today. God will never stop loving any of us, but He does want us to live godly and holy lives before He sends His Son back. Change is not always easy, but it's very necessary.

So are you ready to change or be an agent of change? Because if you and I are going to help people to become overcomers and victors in *any* form of an identity crisis, then surely we have to be free ourselves. But let me say this before I close this chapter. If one of our fellow sisters has lost their identity in this particular area that I've spoken about in regards to homosexuality, we can help them get back on the right track. Galatians 6:1–3 tells us, "Dear brothers and sisters, if another believer is overcome by some sin, you who are godly should gently and humbly help that person back onto the right path. And be careful not to fall into the same temptation yourself. Share each other's burdens, and in this way obey the law of Christ. If you think you are too important to help someone, you are only fooling yourself. You are not that important."

Not only can we help our fellow sisters, but we can help the unsaved as well. We can accomplish this through prayer and the word of God with love and humility. God is interested in saving souls. He's all about relationship and heaven. Will you partner with Him and be an ambassador for Christ?

If you have accepted Christ as your Lord and Savior, walk in freedom. Don't lose sight of who you are in any way right now. Whether you struggle with your identity in regards to self-condemnation, low self-esteem, lack of confidence, what family you were born into, taking on what others say about you, or this issue we just discussed, find your identity in Christ and live free.

SPIRITUAL AFFIRMATIONS

Before we go any further, I'm going to affirm you right now through the power of God's word and encouragement, because that is what He is leading me to do for you at this time. Before I get started, you need to know that the term *affirm* means to state as a fact, assert strongly and publicly, and to offer someone encouragement. So with that being said, I am going to be obedient to His Spirit and do that very thing. Because once you have wholeheartedly accepted Jesus Christ to be Lord and Savior over your life, you can own these words...

You have been adopted into the faith.
You are a child of God.
You are born again.
You have been IDENTIFIED in Christ.
You are valuable.
You have been made righteous through Christ.
You are being changed day by day, and from glory to glory.
You are a new creature.
Old things have passed away. Behold, all things are become new.
Because you have been IDENTIFIED in Christ.
You are who God says you are.
You're not who other people, society, TV,
media, friends, your parents,
or your teachers say you are.
You are everything your Father says you are.
You can have every promise He says you can have.
You can do everything He says you can do.
You have a spiritual inheritance in Christ.
Because you have been IDENTIFIED in Christ.
You are loved by God.
You are adored by Him.
You are His masterpiece.
You are a royal priesthood.
You are a disciple of Christ.
You are a prophetic voice to the nations.
Because you have been IDENTIFIED in Christ.
You are forgiven.

You are redeemed.
You have been called to be set apart.
You are a peculiar person.
You are a citizen of heaven.
You are chosen.
And you have been called for such a time as this
as an **IDENTIFIED** woman in Christ.

Are you receiving these affirmations, sis? I pray that you have been encouraged. Feel free to replace "you" for "I" and encourage yourself with these words. Because you need to know and embrace your value and worth. You need to know that it's high time for you to *know* who you are in Christ like never before, and help others do the same. It's time to get ready to make your spiritual thumbprint in the world for Jesus Christ! Let's do this!

CHAPTER 2

Spiritual Gifts: Identifying Your God-Given Gifts and Calling

"For we are his workmanship, created in Christ Jesus unto good works, which God hath beforehand ordained, that we should walk in them."
—Ephesians 2:10 KJ21

Y ou are God's workmanship! That's right. You are His masterpiece! When He looks at you, He sees something beautiful! He sees the completed work. And He absolutely loves who He created and adopted. Actually, when the Lord created you, He not only placed a measure of faith inside of you to believe in His Son Jesus Christ, but He also knew that He would deposit spiritual gifts and a unique calling within you one day.

Before we move forward, I want to tell you that God wants to use you to do some awesome things to help build His Kingdom. But let me clarify for a moment that it's not by works that you have been saved, yet by His grace and through faith. Salvation is a free gift and there will be no other person, bull, or ram sacrifice that is coming to save us from our sins, because that has already been done through the blood sacrifice of Jesus Christ, our Lord and Savior. Ephesians 2:8-9 states, "For by grace are ye saved through faith; and that not of yourselves: it is a free gift of God. Not of works, lest any man should boast."

So understand that because salvation *is* a free gift, we or others don't have to work our way into heaven. But once we are saved, we *do* have work to do on this earth to help build God's Kingdom. And as we live our Christians lives, we know that God will continue to teach and transform us as we allow Him to, so that we can become greater lights to help win others to Christ through our good works. The Bible shows us that our faith and works go hand-in-hand.

I'm reminded of what James 2:14 tells us, "What good is it, dear brothers and sisters, if you say you have faith but don't show it by your actions? Can that kind of faith save anyone?" Verse 17 goes on to say, "So you see, faith by itself isn't enough. Unless it produces good deeds, it is dead and useless." Remember, Ephesians 2:10 reminds us, "For we are his workmanship, created in Christ Jesus unto good works, which God hath before ordained that we walk in them."

He created and preordained you with a purpose. And knowing these absolute truths should motivate you to leap for joy! It should cause you to put on some praise music and give God a huge shout, "Hallelujah!" Because the reality is that He wants to use *you* to accomplish His great work on this earth. He wants to partner with you to advance the Kingdom of heaven. So, are you up for the challenge?

Trust me. There is nothing like the feeling you get when you know who you are in Christ and begin moving forward in your purpose. It's exhilarating, thought-provoking, challenging at times, and so much more! I'll tell you, even though working for God is all of that, it's worth everything that you have to go through to help others know and live for Jesus.

But before I get ahead of myself in this chapter, first I need to ask you a few questions. Do you know your purpose or calling? Has God given you a dream or vision? Has He placed a passion or burden within you that compels you to want to do something about it? Lastly, have you identified the gifts and talents that the Lord has placed inside of you?

If you know your purpose, spiritual gifts, talents, and what God has called you to do, I think that is totally AWESOME! You are on your way, sis! As you move forward in this book, I'm going to share with you some helpful biblical and practical principles on how to continue walking in your purpose successfully and with the power of the Holy Spirit.

However, for now, let me talk for a minute to the woman who is reading this book but does not quite know her purpose or spiritual gifts yet. Is that you? If it is you, it's okay. Don't panic. I want you to take a minute or two right now and pray. Ask the Lord to reveal His gifts to you, and because I know He is faithful, I believe that He will reveal them to you in His perfect timing.

There is no doubt in my mind that He wants you to know! Remember, He created you for good works and He wants you to do His will. So in the meantime, I want to encourage you to allow the Bible, along with this additional resource, to serve as life-changing guides to lead you in the process of discovery, preparation, and future fulfillment. I also need to say here that whether you know or don't know your gifts and calling, walking in your purpose *is* a process. As a matter of fact, it's a continual one.

In other words, whatever God has called and gifted you to do, it will gradually unfold day by day and step by step. So be patient with yourself and follow the course that God has chosen for you. The Lord will show you how and when to use your gifts. I've definitely learned this over the years.

Personally, God has blessed me with a variety of gifts and talents. He has given me natural talents such as writing, acting, singing, and a little bit of dancing (this one was a shocker for me). He also gifted me with the *motivational gifts* of administration (to put things together, to serve in leadership, etc.) and exhortation. In addition to these spiritual gifts, He also blessed me with the vocational calling to that of an evangelist (i.e., women's speaker). I could list a few more, but the point here is that God has fully equipped me and shown me who I am in Christ. With this knowledge and nearly twenty years of knowing the Lord, combined with training and life experiences, I have moved forward in my purpose while helping others do the same.

Just to give a brief illustration of how gifts operate within your calling, I'll share with you how the Lord uses the gift of writing to help me encourage and minister to others. This will hopefully give you a glimpse of how it works in real life. I have used my heavenly gift of writing for blogging and writing magazine articles, plays, skits, press releases, professional letters, business plans, marketing and public relations campaigns, social media promos, and now books. I absolutely love what God does through this gift. He has even opened the door for speaking engagements through my writing as well.

Now, I must say that even though He deposited this special talent inside of me during creation, it didn't come out as soon as I was born. And it certainly hasn't been a flower bed of ease using it. There has definitely been a process of preparation, education, exposure, cultivation, purification, and challenge. Having said that, my English and Bible teachers, spiritual leaders, and my mom have all played vital roles in the process of honing my craft. But the Holy Spirit played the most critical role of all.

It all started when my mom bought me my first diary. Immediately, as a little girl, I fell in love with the pen and notebook. My mother also used to take me and my little sister to local bookstores, and that's when I developed a love for reading books. I undeniably loved going to the bookstore! I still do. It's one of my favorite hangouts.

I also enjoyed writing creative stories and bringing words to life. I remember one day when my super fun Uncle Robert read one of my creative little books I had authored at the tender age of twelve. He shouted, "You should write a book!" Well, if he were still alive today, I think he would be proud that his words actually came true. *You're reading one of them.*

Another incredible real-life example is that I've always wanted to work and write for a magazine company. Well, Jesus opened that door for me years ago to work for one, and now (at the time of this writing), I am a contributing writer for several magazines! Isn't the Lord marvelous? The Bible tells us in Proverbs 18:16, "A man's gift maketh room for him, and bringeth him before great men." This wise proverb works for us women, too!

The point here is that once you discover and know your gifts and calling, guess what? **Your identity will be even more defined.** Life will become even more exciting and interesting once you know a little bit more about yourself. Knowing your gifts will give you that extra vigor when you wake up in the morning saying, "Good morning, Lord!" Now, you'll be able to add, "Lord, how can I be used for your glory today?"

He wants to use you in this end time generation, sis. Again, He has called you for such a time as this. So knowing your identity in Christ is huge. Knowing your gifts is big. And walking in your calling is simply GIGANTIC! But before you start moving forward towards your divine destiny, let's talk more specifically about *identifying* your spiritual gifts and calling, so you will have what you need to bring others into the Kingdom and encourage the body of Christ until Jesus returns!

IDENTIFYING YOUR SPIRITUAL GIFTS

It's important to identify your spiritual gifts, so that you know not only your makeup but also how to flow and function, specifically in the body of Christ. What that means is that we, the church, make up the body of Christ. And Jesus is our head. He is our humble leader. With that being said, the Holy Spirit has gifted each one of us uniquely, so that we are able to serve one another well, as we lead others to accept and live for Christ. Got it?

Okay. Let's go a little deeper. Get your highlighter and pen ready, because you're about to become more enlightened on the spiritual gifts. You're about to embark upon the special abilities that the Holy Spirit grants to each of us. The Bible, in 1 Corinthians 12:7 says, "A spiritual gift is given to each of us so we can help each other." Meaning, so we can all benefit from it.

As you read through the upcoming verses, try identifying or confirming what gifts the Holy Spirit has given to you. Ready? It says in 1 Corinthians 12:8–10, "To one person the Spirit gives the ability to give wise advice, to another the same Spirit gives a message of special knowledge. The same Spirit gives great faith to another, and to someone else the one Spirit gives the gift of healing. He gives one person the power to perform miracles, and another the ability to prophesy. He gives someone else the ability to discern whether a message is from the Spirit of God or from another spirit. Still another person is given the ability to speak in unknown languages, while another is given the ability to interpret what is being said."

For clarity purposes, I'm going to break this passage of Scripture down into bite-sized pieces. As you read, see which gifts you possess through the Holy Spirit. The first one is a word of wisdom. The second one is a word of knowledge. Next up is the gift of faith. Another is the gift of healing. A different one is the gift to perform miracles. The following one is to prophesy or give a prophetic word. Then there's the gift of discernment (i.e., being able to tell right from wrong or good from evil). The last two gifts in this vein are the abilities to speak in unknown tongues and to interpret what is being said through unknown tongues.

Now, read and listen with spiritual eyes and ears to what 1 Corinthians 12:11 declares, "It is the one and only Spirit who distributes all these gifts. He alone decides which gift each person should have." This verse lets you know to be alert. So be careful not to let others define or dictate who they may want you to be. You have the ability to discover who you are. They may take a guess at it, but the Lord needs to confirm it. Remember, the Holy Spirit is the only one who distributes these gifts to you.

To bring further understanding to this truth, I believe it's safe to say that He will use others to encourage you to flow in them, as well as train you to operate in them effectively. Also, your spiritual leaders in your church will be able to assist you in this process. But again, the Holy Spirit is the only one who gives them to you.

My advice would be to pray and ask the Holy Spirit to show you clearly. I believe wholeheartedly that He is faithful to reveal and confirm your gifts to you. A great book that I want to recommend to you at this time is entitled, *Discover Your God-Given Gifts*, by Don and Katie Fortune. Grab this book!

It's totally awesome as it relates to helping you identify your spiritual gifts. There's a great breakdown of each gift, as well as a test incorporated throughout the book. Personally, I think it is fun discovering who you truly are through this mix of gifts that the Spirit of God grants. Here's a bit of advice. Once you discover them, learn how to use them to better serve others well. Keep in mind, we want to hear one day, "Well done, thou good and faithful servant," (Matthew 25:21 KJ21).

Before I move on to talk about identifying your God-given calling, I want to share a few more spiritual gifts. See if you can identify yourself as these questions are asked in 1 Peter 4:11, "Do you have the gift of speaking?" YES! I do! Sorry, I got excited! Okay, let's proceed.

Peter goes on to say, "Then speak as though God himself were speaking through you." Amen! He continues, "Do you have the gift of helping others? Do it with all the strength and energy that God supplies. Then everything you do will bring glory to God through Jesus Christ. All glory and power to him forever and ever! Amen." So do you see yourself in any of these gifts? If not, no pressure. But if you do, highlight it, take note, and allow God to show you how to use them well.

Romans 12:6–8 reveals, "In his grace, God has given us different gifts for doing certain things well. So if God has given you the ability to prophesy, speak out with as much faith as God has given you. If your gift is serving others, serve them well. If you are a teacher, teach well. If your gift is to encourage others, be encouraging. If it is giving, give generously. If God has given you leadership ability, take the responsibility seriously. And if you have the gift of showing kindness to others, do it gladly."

In a nutshell, this is how these gifts are described:

- prophesy (perceiver)
- service (server)
- teaching (teacher)
- exhortation (exhorter)
- giving (giver)
- leadership (administrator)
- mercy (compassion)

Can you identify with these gifts? Again, the book I recommended earlier in this chapter will help you gain a better understanding of these in clarity and detail. Hopefully, what I've shared so far is beginning to spark something fresh and exciting inside of you! I pray that it will put a charge in you that makes you want to use your gifts in the church and beyond! I also pray that this book will help you to flow in your gift with a God confidence. We'll talk more about that in a later chapter. But for now, we're going to move into identifying your calling.

IDENTIFYING YOUR CALLING

I'm going to jump right into this one! Do you know what you're called to do? Do you know what you were put on this earth to accomplish? Are you preparing for it or operating in it? Or are you still trying to figure it out? In either case, there are two sides to this reality. Either you know or you're trying to find out.

I've been on both sides. At first, I didn't know. But then one day, I prayed and asked the Lord, "What is my purpose?" And later, "Who am I?" From then on, my purpose began to unfold and the Lord showed me who I am in Christ.

I am a child of God. I am a mother and a wife. I am also a writer and speaker. I have been given the gift of evangelism. He has given me a burden and a heart to help women grow in their walk with Him. I am IDENTIFIED. And I make my boast in the Lord, because it is only by the grace of God that I am able to do any of these amazing things. I'm forever humbled and grateful.

Listen, sis. Wherever you are, God will show you what He is calling you to do and how to operate in it. As a matter of fact, He will show you step by step and from faith unto faith how to walk in your calling effectively. Be patient, for as Matthew 7:7–8 assures us, "Keep on asking, and you will receive what you ask for. Keep on seeking, and you will find. Keep on knocking, and the door will be opened to you. For everyone who asks, receives. Everyone who seeks, finds. And to everyone who knocks, the door will be opened." In the meantime, let's talk more in detail about identifying your calling.

What has God been showing you lately? What has He been leading you to do? Have you seen a pattern? Do you have a passion for something? Again, has He shown you a dream or a vision? Has He placed a burden in your heart?

Do you feel led to do prison ministry, to help orphans or children with single parents, or maybe volunteer in the mission field? Are you called to use your gifts to sing, teach, dance, write, or lead? Has God called you to start a non-profit organization, business, or ministry? Has He called you to work a secular job to impact those in your workplace? All of these are examples of callings, and there are so many more! The list could literally go on and on. God will show you what you are called to do. He will also use others in leadership to help you. So you're not alone in this process.

Here's another great way to identify who you are. Consider these thought-provoking questions that I'm borrowing from the gifts portion of this chapter. See if you can identify yourself in any of these. (NOTE: You will *not* have all of them, but ask the Holy Spirit to reveal which ones you identify with.)

1. Are you a perceiver?
2. Are you a server?
3. Are you a teacher?
4. Are you an exhorter?
5. Are you a giver?
6. Are you an administrator or leader?
7. Are you very compassionate?
8. Do you speak in tongues?
9. Do you interpret tongues?
10. Do you have the gift of faith?
11. Do you have the gift of healing?
12. Do you have the gift of giving a word of wisdom?
13. Do you have the gift of giving a word of knowledge?
14. Do you have the gift to perform miracles?

15. Do you have the gift to prophesy?
16. Do you have the gift to discern spirits?
17. Do you have the gift of helping?
18. Do you believe the Lord has called you to the "five-fold ministry?" Meaning do you sense the calling on your life to be a pastor, teacher, apostle, prophet, or evangelist?

Did you identify yourself in any of these gifts and callings? I need to mention here that even though this list is long, and maybe even a little overwhelming, don't be intimidated. Not everyone possesses all of these gifts. It's important to know that God will only give what each of us needs to accomplish His plan and purpose.

Paul confirms this in 1 Corinthians 12:29–30, "Are we all apostles? Are we all prophets? Are we all teachers? Do we all have the power to do miracles? Do we all have the gift of healing? Do we all have the ability to speak in unknown languages? Do we all have the ability to interpret unknown languages? Of course not!" See. We don't have it all. That's why it's important to pray and ask the Lord to show you clearly who you are, and to do what Paul states in 1 Corinthians 12:31, "So you should earnestly desire the most helpful gifts." The whole purpose in this, is so you can be more effective in helping others as you operate in your calling.

Before I close this chapter, for clarity purposes, let me speak a little bit about the five-fold ministry. Jesus is the One who gives these vocational gifts. Ephesians 4:11–12 states, "Now these are the gifts Christ gave to the church: the apostles, the prophets, the evangelists, and the pastors and teachers. Their responsibility is to equip God's people to do His work and build up the church, the body of Christ."

Again, not everyone is called to *these* particular callings. Think about it, you can't have twenty pastors in one church, unless you have a huge congregation. But even still, someone has to lead and shepherd all of the members. For instance, there weren't twenty Moseses, there was only one Moses. Aaron and the others under Moses were appointed leaders with different responsibilities. But again, there was only one Moses.

Trust me. I know there are associate pastors and elders, and that the church appoints positions such as a youth pastor, worship pastor, missions pastor, etc. These are all callings, but I hope you understand the main point here. Everyone *can't* operate as a pastor, teacher, apostle, prophet, and evangelist. If everyone in the church filled these particular roles, the body of Christ would be in total chaos! There would be absolutely no order. Who would be following? If half the church members were evangelists, there wouldn't be many people to teach or shepherd. They would all be out of town traveling. Get the point? So know for a fact if any of these are your calling or someone else's. There are plenty of gifts to go around for everyone.

I also need to note here that God will fully equip you to operate in any area of your calling. He will prepare you in a variety of ways. In addition, be sure to pray and ask for assistance from your spiritual leaders and godly counsel. Seek help through biblical courses, either online or offline, at your church, conferences, books, and especially the Bible. There is no doubt in my mind that the Lord will help you in every way to walk out your calling successfully.

KNOWING YOUR SPIRITUAL GIFTS AND GOD-GIVEN CALLING

Knowing your spiritual gifts and calling is only half the battle. I say that because sometimes God will call you to do some things that will be easygoing, and sometimes He will ask you to do things that will be tough. I know this from experience. Personally, I haven't always liked doing some of the things that God has asked me to do. Some things were really hard. Some things I didn't even understand. Not to mention the spiritual warfare that comes with it.

BUT, in spite of it all, I managed to press through my inability, while relying on His supernatural ability to accomplish His will. One verse that helps me as I do the work of the Lord is when God speaks in Zechariah 4:6 saying, "'Not by might, nor by power, but by my spirit,' saith the LORD of hosts" (KJ21). I've learned that the way to get things done is by the power of God's Holy Spirit. We can do nothing that really counts towards heaven without His power.

I'll tell you, when my difficult assignments were all said and done, all I could do was give God all the praise and glory! I knew that it was nobody but Him that accomplished them. I was just a vessel. So keep in mind that as God begins to use you, some things will be hard to respond, "Yes, Lord!" But you can know for sure that when you trust and rely on Him, He will get the job done—by His Spirit!

I need to say something. Jesus did a lot of things. He was a carpenter. He taught, healed, cast out demons, and performed many miracles. But Calvary was hard. We know this because we've read it in the Scriptures. Jesus went to His Father, pleading with Him to take that cup away. Yet, in spite of that tough call on His life, He pressed forward and did it! He did it for you and for me, and for so many others. He did it because it was God's will. He did it because He loves us. And that's the key—*love*.

As we walk out our calling through the variety of gifts that the Lord and His precious Holy Spirit have given us, let us be sure of our calling and walk in humility, peace, and love. The Bible warns us that without love, we have nothing. Paul confirms this in 1 Corinthians 13:1–3 saying, "If I could speak all the languages of earth and of angels, but didn't love others, I would only be a noisy gong or a clanging cymbal. If I had the gift of prophecy, and I understood all of God's secret plans and possessed all knowledge, and if I had such faith that I could move mountains, but didn't love others, I would be nothing. If I gave everything I have to the poor and even sacrificed my body, I could boast about it; but if I didn't love others, I would have gained nothing."

My sister, without love, we have nothing. Meaning, if we possess those amazing gifts that we've been talking about, but have not love, the Bible tells us that we have gained nothing. All of those works become worthless. We work in vain.

I don't know if you've ever noticed, but there is nothing like seeing a Christian operate in gifts and talents without love. It's disheartening. Actually, I think we all could use a good heart check in this area, truth be told. If we're ever operating *without* love, we need to go to the throne room of grace and ask the Lord to forgive us of this sin, because that is exactly what it is. The world can't see the light of Jesus if we are not walking in love with one another and towards others. We are called to love.

God is serious about love. And thank God there's hope. This is how we can demonstrate charity with our gifts and callings. We read in 1 Corinthians 13:4–7, "Love is patient and kind. Love is not jealous or boastful or proud or rude. It does not demand its own way. It is not irritable, and it keeps no record of being wronged. It does not rejoice about injustice but rejoices whenever the truth wins out. Love never gives up, never loses faith, is always hopeful, and endures through every circumstance." This is love in action with our gifts and callings.

The truth of the matter is that if we are going to flow in our purpose, especially as leaders in the church, but also as the body of Christ, then we *need* to be reminded of what Paul instructs us to do in Ephesians 4:1–5, "Therefore I, a prisoner for serving the Lord, beg you to lead a life worthy of your calling, for you have been called by God. Always be humble and gentle. Be patient with each other, making allowance for each other's faults because of your love.

Make every effort to keep yourselves united in the Spirit, binding yourselves together with peace. For there is one body and one Spirit, just as you have been called to one glorious hope for the future. There is one Lord, one faith, one baptism, and one God and Father of all, who is over all, in all, and living through all."

Jesus was love in action. And as His followers, we are called to act the same way. He was also grace in the realist form. He was a humble leader, and He was so patient. But He also knew who He was when He walked this earth, and still today. He knew His calling. He knew His purpose. Now, He wants you to know yours and walk in it.

As I prepare to close this chapter, Jesus wants you to accomplish the Father's will, and to know that the Kingdom of God is within you. My sister, you have the power inside of you to do great things for the Lord. The Holy Spirit dwells within you. Can you sense that? I pray that you do.

The Lord wants to use your gifts, your talents, your calling to help encourage and build up your church, community, workplace, home environment, social media network, and beyond! Know that whom He calls, He also fully equips. Now let me operate in my gifting to write to you and encourage you with God's word in Ephesians 3:20–21, "Now all glory to God, who is able, through his mighty power at work within us, to accomplish infinitely more than we might ask or think. Glory to him in the church and in Christ Jesus through all generations forever and ever! Amen." I love you, sis.

Now let's move forward…

CHAPTER 3

Spiritual Preparation: Discipleship and Personal Discipline

"Jesus called out to them, 'Come, follow me, and
I will show you how to fish for people!' And they
left their nets at once and followed Him."
—MATTHEW 4:19-20

J esus is calling out to you, too. He is saying, "Follow me." No matter how long you have been saved, He wants you to follow Him with everything inside of you, NOW. I have prayed for you, my sister. I cried out, "Lord, you know where each woman is that will be reading this book. Speak to her." So it is not by chance that you are reading this book or looking over these lines at this very moment.

Jesus has chosen you. He has called you. And He has IDENTIFIED you as His disciple. And now, He wants to show you how to fish for people. So will you drop everything at once to focus on following Jesus faithfully as you prepare to walk out your divine calling?

Because now that you are His disciple (i.e., a follower of Christ), He has called you to come and learn how be a part of His amazing plan in winning souls during these last days of harvest. John the Baptist and the disciples in Jesus' day were witnesses of His arrival and departure. But you and I, my dear sister, will be the disciples and witnesses of declaring His return. He wants to use your gifts and talents to do what He has commissioned you to do in this latter day generation. Can you sense it?

The world is in turmoil. Many people are lost and in need of a Savior. That's why God sent His Son. And that's why He's also spiritually preparing you to point them back toward Him. Just to give you a quick, sisterhood reminder, the Bible states, "For God so loved the world that he gave his only begotten Son, that whosoever believeth in him should not perish, but have everlasting life" (John 3:16 KJ21). God doesn't want anyone in this world to perish.

Actually, the only reason why Jesus hasn't returned yet (at the time of this writing) is because the Bible says that God is being patient. In 2 Peter 3:9–10 it says, "The Lord isn't really being slow about his promise, as some people think. No, he is being patient for your sake. He does not want anyone to be destroyed, but wants everyone to repent. But the day of the Lord will come as unexpectedly as a thief. Then the heavens will pass away with a terrible noise, and the very elements themselves will disappear in fire, and the earth and everything on it will be found to deserve judgment." So you see. He doesn't want anyone to perish or miss the opportunity to experience the beautiful life that's forthcoming. He doesn't want anyone to miss heaven and the New Jerusalem! But He also doesn't want people to experience His judgment.

That's why He's waiting...*patiently*. And that's love. Even while many people are scoffing at His word right now. Yet, the Bible warns us that scoffers will come in the last days. Second Peter 3:3–4 states, "Most importantly, I want to remind you that in the last days scoffers will come, mocking the truth and following their own desires. They will say, 'What happened to the promise that Jesus is coming again? From before the time of our ancestors, everything has remained the same since the world was first created.'"

That's what scoffers look like. Simply stated, they are individuals who mock God's word and His followers. They tend to question and cast doubt on what the Bible actually says. So have you experienced any scoffers lately? I have. When I encounter them, I tell them about this verse. Because God is not slack about His promise. Jesus IS coming back. And when He comes, it will be swift and with judgment! But that's where we come in.

Jesus has called you and me as end time warriors to help. He has called us to advance the Kingdom of heaven by reeling the world in...before it's too late. He has called us to fish for souls. Remember, we were once a part of this world, but God loved us so much that He sent His Son, and used others to help reel us in. That's His love in action. But in His love, He is also calling for repentance from everyone. Today is the day of salvation. Today is the day to be IDENTIFIED.

The clock is winding down. The hour is late. That's why we, as born again believers, do not have time to lose sight of who we are in Christ right now. We are His true disciples. We are called, and we have to stand firm on these facts as we focus on what He has commissioned us to do, which is to be fishers of men, but also to, "Go and make disciples" (Matthew 28:18–20).

With that being said, we must first prepare. We must practice discipleship. And we must have personal discipline as we move forward in our purpose to win souls for the Kingdom. In this chapter, I'm going to talk specifically to these key points. Because I believe it's important for us as disciples to have a healthy helping of God's word. We also need to have a consistent prayer life. And we must develop personal discipline as we do what the Lord has called us to do. We have to be spiritually fit and prepared to walk out our destiny. So let's talk about it.

SPIRITUAL PREPARATION: DISCIPLESHIP

In a brief synopsis, discipleship is mainly about spiritual growth through biblical teaching. Notice when Jesus called the disciples, He also taught them. He didn't just leave them to learn how to walk out this life on their own. He was their Master and their humble Teacher, and He is the same for us today.

Even though He is our Master and Teacher, God also sends us trained messengers here on earth. Pastors, teachers, evangelists, apostles, and prophets are called to humbly teach, train, equip, and encourage us in our walks as Christians. In addition, the Lord uses authors, bloggers, and speakers, as well as tools, schools, Bible studies, and many other resources to aid in our spiritual development. All of this encompasses discipleship.

The root word *disciple* is really defined as a follower of Jesus Christ, and one who embraces and assists in spreading the teaching of another. The term *discipleship* is defined as being in the position of a disciple, and the process of embracing the life and ethics of Jesus Christ because of the hope laid out in the Gospel. Walking out your calling is going to be a process—even as it relates to discipleship.

So as you prepare to move forward in your purpose, understand that discipleship must be a key component in your spiritual life. Because if you are going to be helping other people, then you are going to have to make sure that you are rooted and grounded in the word of God. In saying this, I need to pause here to ask you a few questions. Do you have a church home? If so, that's great! But if you don't, pray and ask the Lord to lead you to a good Bible-believing church that stands wholeheartedly on the full counsel of the word of God. My next question is, are you in a weekly Bible study or discipleship class?

The reason why I ask these questions is because staying connected to the Vine (which is Jesus) and the word of God in various ways is going to be so vital for your spiritual growth. Don't get me wrong, Sunday morning service is phenomenal! But you need more. And that more is discipleship.

Notice in the Gospels of Matthew, Mark, Luke, and John, and even the beginning of the book of Acts, the disciples wanted more of Jesus. They would *not* settle for experiencing Him once a week. They wanted Him daily. Granted, this does not mean that you have to be inside the church every time the doors are open, but the point here is that when you hunger and thirst after God and His righteousness, Jesus teaches us that we shall be filled as Matthew 5:6 encourages. And that's a blessing!

Think about it this way. When you're hungry, and I mean, really hungry, quite naturally, you are going to hunt for food. Whether that is in your pantry, refrigerator, local restaurant, or the nearest fast-food chain that you can drive or walk to—you just want to eat! You want to fill that desire, right? Well, that's what discipleship in action feels like. You are hungry for truth, and you want more of God. Actually, it's probably more like a desire for dessert! It's that craving you get when you just want to fulfill that sweet tooth. King David stated how sweet God's word is in Psalm 119:103, "How sweet your words taste to me; they are sweeter than honey." Have you ever thought about discipleship in this way? It's just so good!

Let me give you a few practical ways to take advantage of discipleship opportunities. If your church has a mid-week service, go. Check it out and receive the message that the Lord wants to give you for that week. Is there a women's ministry or women's Bible study that is conducted at your church during the week? If so, sign up, go, and grow. You can attend a women's group or women's conference that may be happening in your area. You might even want to join a book club or start a six-week devotional over coffee with your girlfriends. I'm just giving you a few experiential suggestions of how you can not only connect, worship, and fellowship with other like-minded believers, but also grow and enjoy your life as a Christian woman.

Personally, I like discipleship classes, and I *love* women's fellowships and conferences, as well as worship concerts. The conferences and concerts are great refreshers for me. And the discipleship classes nurture my spiritual maturity on a weekly basis. I not only need it, but I also take pleasure in it. I often tell people how much I love and enjoy my Christian life!

Hopefully, you're already plugged into a weekly regimen of Bible study and fellowship. But if you're not, I pray that you will get connected soon for your own spiritual health and maturity. Remember, it's vital to grow as a Christ-follower. Not only that, but when you do this for yourself, you'll be amazed at how easy it will be to encourage someone else to do the same. It's all about contagious living. And discipleship is key!

SPIRITUAL PREPARATION:
PERSONAL DISCIPLINE

I would venture to humbly say that many women are going to like this part (hopefully, you included), because it deals with not only personal discipline, but also balance and wisdom as it relates to doing what God has called us to do. In my experience, I have had many women request more on this topic of balance. In this section, I'm going to break down these specific areas:

- Prayer
- Devotion
- Reading and studying God's word effectively
- Memorizing and meditating on Scripture
- Planning your weekly schedule
- Managing stress, anxiety, and frustration

- Taking care of your home life
- The power of agreement
- Exercising and maintaining a healthy nutritional plan

So let's begin.

Prayer – For starters, I could not do any of this without prayer. It is my lifeline! Actually, it's a lifeline for both of us, sis! There is no way that you can successfully move forward into your purpose without it. It would be operating in the flesh instead of walking in the Spirit. If you're going to attempt to do great things for God, or His will, then you must have a prayer life. Jesus had a rich prayer life. And you are His follower, so follow suit. The King James Version in 1 Thessalonians 5:17 says, "Pray without ceasing." In the New Living Translation version it strongly states, "Never stop praying." Again, it's your lifeline. If you want to know what God wants you to do, or if you need wisdom in anything, then you're going to need to stay connected through prayer. James 1:5 reminds us, "If you need wisdom, ask our generous God, and he will give it to you. He will not rebuke you for asking." So keep praying, and as the Lord leads you, consider fasting as well.

Fasting is a great way to sacrifice your natural comforts such as food, to hear more clearly from God in specific areas in your life. For instance, if you need direction, wisdom, answers on something, or just simply desire to be closer to God and deeper in His presence, this is a great spiritual discipline. The Bible records in Matthew 4:2 that Jesus fasted and prayed before He started His earthly ministry. So it's totally okay. A few helpful suggestions on what types of fasts you can do are: a one-day fast (no food, just juice and water), twelve-hour fast (e.g., 6 a.m. to 6 p.m., no food, just juice and water), a two or three-day fast (with limited diet or no food, just juice and water), or a forty-day Daniel Fast (this fast is done with food, but the menu is modified—mainly with fruit, veggies, and water). I want to caution you to check with your doctor or health professional before you embark upon a fast if you have a previous medical condition. But no matter your health condition, fasting should be done with wisdom. A book that I highly recommend that breaks down this particular spiritual discipline is entitled, *Fasting: Opening the door to a deeper, more intimate, more powerful relationship with God* by Jentezen Franklin. I pray this all helps.

Devotion – Do you have a daily regimen devoting quiet time to be alone with God and in His word? If you don't have that time yet, don't feel bad about it. Just pray and ask the Lord to help you find that moment in your day to spend with Him. You have to stay connected. Purpose in your heart to do it, and keep it. Carving out this precious time in your day is crucial for your spiritual walk. Think about it. It's your devotion and your love toward Him demonstrated in real life. I'm reminded of the story of Mary and Martha in the Bible. Remember Martha? She was so busy getting everything ready to please the Lord, that she missed spending time with Him. Martha even became indignant with Jesus saying, "Lord, doesn't it seem unfair to you that my sister just sits here while I do all the work? Tell her to come and help me" (Luke 10:40). Martha tried to tell Jesus what to do. But this was His answer, "My dear Martha, you are worried and upset over all these details! There is only one thing worth being concerned about. Mary has discovered it, and it will not be taken away from her" (Luke 10:41–42). Wow! Amen Jesus! How often are we so busy doing things *for* God, or concerned about what others are *not* doing, that we miss stopping and spending time with Him ourselves? I know that I am guilty of busyness at times. I literally have to stop and remind myself that I need to spend time supping with Him. Have you ever been guilty of busyness? Have you ever put His work or your natural job before Him? We must make sure to keep our priorities in order as we stay devoted to Him. Remember, it's also about a having relationship. Another good book that I want to recommend to you is entitled, *Having a Mary Heart in a Martha World* by Joanna Weaver.

Reading and studying God's word effectively – It's good to have a designated time to read your Bible. This can, of course, happen during your devotional time. However, it can also occur when you're about to go to bed, or while listening to an audio app of the Bible as you cook, clean, fix your hair and makeup, or while you're driving into work. Reading the word has gotten so much easier over the years. Praise God! Romans 10:17 tells us, "So then faith cometh by hearing, and hearing by the word of God" (KJ21). So read it, speak it, and listen to it. But not only that, study it. Second Timothy 2:15 instructs us saying, "Study to show thyself approved unto God, a workman who needeth not to be ashamed, rightly dividing the word of truth" (KJ21). This is one of my life Scriptures. As a teacher of God's word and a writer, this is crucial for me—yet for you as well. We are both instructed to study the word so that we can not only know it and be approved by God, but also to rightly break it down so that others can understand it as well. When we take the time to do this, we can be unashamed of the gospel and go forth boldly in His truth. So let's keep studying the word, that way we can effectively do what the Lord has called us to do. Amen!

Memorizing and meditating on Scripture – I love the book of Joshua. Actually, when I asked the Lord who I could most identify with in the Bible, He whispered to me many years ago, "Joshua." Ever since that day, the words, "Be strong and courageous," have resonated with me. These words have been life-giving! Because this message related to the fact that even though God had called Joshua to do some big, yet tough things, He was letting Joshua know in advance that He was going to be right there with him wherever he would go. When I first read that, it increased my faith BIG TIME!

I hope it does the same for you. But that's not all He told Joshua. God also told him, "Study this Book of Instruction continually. Meditate on it day and night so you will be sure to obey everything written in it. Only then will you prosper and succeed in all you do" (Joshua 1:8). If you want to be prosperous and successful, follow the word that was spoken to Joshua. This word still stands true for us today. You and I are called to meditate on Scripture. And memorizing it practically seals it in our hearts. King David wrote in Psalm 119:11, "I have hidden your word in my heart, that I might not sin against you." Memorizing and meditating on the word of God is a powerful and life-changing practice as it relates to spiritual preparation and personal discipline.

By the way, who do you identify with in the Bible? For instance, personally, over the years I've been able to identify with Joshua, Paul, John the Baptist, and Nehemiah. In different seasons of my life, their life examples have helped me complete assignments, be bold and courageous, and accomplish much! So think about that for a minute.

Planning your weekly schedule - The next thing as it relates to personal discipline is having an organized daily or weekly schedule. Proper preparation will do wonders for you as you go about doing what God has called you to do in this season. There is no way that I could work through my week without the Holy Spirit leading and guiding me, and also my weekly planner. If you don't have a day planner, then I highly suggest that you buy one. You can even use an electronic calendar or task list on your phone, but the point here is to get one! The planner's sole purpose is to help you lay out your work week (and/or day), and just flow! You don't want to fly by the seat of your pants as you do the will of God. Your planner will help you set some order in your work day. Personally, I like to fill my planner with a study or devotional time to kick off my day, and then I lay out my goals through a one page To-Do List. I have all of my *high priorities* categorized and listed as HP1, HP2, HP3, etc. After I identify these priorities on my list, everything else just follows. But this helps me keep things in order and proper perspective. That's how things get done! As for you, feel free to create your own To-Do List as you feel most comfortable. Over the years, I have had many ways of laying out my schedule for my work week, but I've finally found my rhythm. Whatever you do, plan. Planning your schedule for the day or week (while also keeping in mind that God is fully in control and can alter your schedule at any time!) will help alleviate undue stress, keep things in order, and prioritize, so you can accomplish much! But as you do all of this, keep in mind what Proverbs 16:9 says, "We can make our plans, but the Lord determines our steps." Keep it all in perspective and don't forget to pray for a productive week!

Managing stress, anxiety, and frustrations – For starters, stress and anxiety are just not good physically, mentally, or spiritually. And when you're frustrated about things, it's best to just take a step back and begin trusting the Holy Spirit to take the lead. This takes a conscious effort on your part. Specifically, if you've been feeling a little stressed out lately, I encourage you to pray and seek wisdom on ways to alleviate it. Because unmanaged stress and anxiety can make you sick, make you feel like you're going to have a heart attack, or put you in the hospital. Worse than that, stress and anxiety can stagnate your progress! That can be a work of the enemy right there, trying to stop you or distract you, possibly convincing you to try and work in your own strength and ability. Remember what God says in Zechariah 4:6, "It's by my Spirit, saith the Lord of hosts" (KJV). So calm down. Relax. Breathe. Renew your thoughts and allow the Holy Spirit to give you peace of mind. Remember, you are not alone in the process. Let His Spirit work *through* you. Don't worry and don't be anxious. Philippians 4:6–7 says, "Don't worry about anything; instead, pray about everything.

Tell God what you need, and thank him for all he has done. Then you will experience God's peace, which exceeds anything we can understand. His peace will guard your hearts and minds as you live in Christ Jesus." Let His peace work. And don't forget to thank Him along the way.

Taking care of your home life – How's the home front? Whether you are single, engaged, married with kids or not, God wants you to keep it all in balance, sis. I know that might be tough at times, but with God, all things are possible! It's true. And this doesn't mean that you have to have a perfectly swept, spotlessly clean, picture-perfect house or apartment with gourmet meals cooked every night. Yet, there does need to be some order and cleanliness and prepared nourishment while you grind. Meaning, as you do God's will, you've got to keep things in order. You must have clean clothes, clean dishes, and clean children (if you have them). And your loved ones have to eat, sis! I hope you're getting the point. The angle here is that you are called to be a godly example to others. There are other women who are watching you, whether you realize it or believe it. And some need the word of your testimony to see how they can obtain balance, too. So as an older woman (with younger women watching), you are called also to be a light to them. Now I'm not calling you old, but you're older than someone, hun! Titus 2:4–5 says, "These older women must train the younger women to love their husbands and their children, to live wisely and be pure, to work in their homes, to do good, and to be submissive to their husbands. Then they will not bring shame on the word of God." He's got you. Don't feel anxious or stressed out about this (we already covered that part). Yet, it *is* something to allow the Holy Spirit to help you work through, as you walk in your purpose. He will give you the strength. It's time to shine bright inside the house and beyond! Women are watching.

The power of agreement – I think the power of agreement is very important as it relates to personal discipline and as you prepare to move forward in your purpose. I would also add consultation. Pray, ask, and consult God before you accept any assignment or request from your job or ministry. I say this because you want to make sure that it *really* is a God-ordained assignment or position, and not something that either you or the enemy has cooked up. Just make sure you consult the Lord before you move forward. Be sure to seek godly counsel as well. Proverbs 15:22 says, "Plans go wrong for lack of advice; many advisers bring success." I have been here before, and I can assure you there is peace when you follow God's word and seek wise godly counsel. Again, make sure that God is the one leading you with whatever you are doing, and if you're married, make sure that your hubby is in agreement as well. It just grants you so much peace in the long run.

Exercising and maintaining a healthy nutritional plan – Let me start by confessing that I am not in love with working out (even though I am married to a fitness trainer and gym owner). Phew, it feels good to be honest! Nonetheless, that does not change the fact that I must take care of my body. And so do you. Yep! We've got to do it, sis. We only have one temple. And the Holy Spirit dwells there. With all of this being said, I encourage you, just as I encourage myself, to work out—exercise, my sister! There are all sorts of programs out there that can assist you as you press towards reaching your fitness goals and ideal weight. And don't forget about implementing a healthy eating pattern as well. It will help you not only lose excess and unwanted fat, but it will also help you maintain your weight once you reach your goal. My hubby likes to say, "It's a lifestyle, not a diet plan." So proper exercise, accompanied with a healthy nutritional plan and a good multivitamin, will do wonders for your endurance and overall health. Yes, it will take personal discipline, but it can be accomplished. Think about it this way—God will give you *and* me the strength and willpower to get it done. Help us, Lord!

SPIRITUALLY PREPARED

I pray that these biblical and practical nuggets have been helpful to you. The whole purpose for this chapter was to help you realize that you have to be spiritually prepared and fit to walk in your calling successfully. Remember, Jesus has called *you* to follow Him to win souls for heaven! Knowing this, you want to make sure that you have the spiritual and natural stamina to accomplish this great task. Diligent preparation through discipleship and personal discipline will help big time!

I hope that you'll begin putting these things into practice. Only you and God know which Bible studies you need to attend, what time is a good time to read, memorize, and study His word, and which fitness program is right for your body. The lesson here is to teach you about spiritual growth and how to develop a more consistent plan for your journey toward your purpose. These tools will help you become spiritually prepared.

Again, God wants to use you in these last days for His glory and to increase His Kingdom. He will fully equip you to get it done! Knowing this great fact should bring joy to your soul. I want to share something with you before I close this chapter. I can recall getting dressed in a women's dressing room several years ago, and I remember as I looked in the mirror, the Lord whispered to me, "I will fully equip you."

Undoubtedly, I knew it was Him! When I looked in the mirror, He knew where my heart and mind were at the time—He knew that I was thinking about my purpose. And now, I'm walking in it! But first He had to fully equip and spiritually prepare me for it.

So I just want to encourage you, my sister. God knows where you are. He knows your heart and your deepest thoughts. He knows your passions and innermost desires. And He knows the burden that He's placed inside of your heart to do what He has called you to do. Psalms 139:1–5 confirms this by saying, "O LORD, you have examined my heart and know everything about me. You know when I sit down or stand up. You know my thoughts even when I'm far away. You see me when I travel and when I rest at home. You know everything I do. You know what I am going to say even before I say it, LORD. You go before me and follow me. You place your hand of blessing on my head." He's got you covered, sis!

With that being said, let Him fully equip you through His word. He will give you everything you need for your calling. You can count on that truth! Personally, I know it to be true in my own life. The Scripture says in Psalm 119:105, "Your word is a lamp to guide my feet and a light for my path." This particular verse has really come alive in my life, and it has the power to do the same for you! The Bible and the Holy Spirit will be your compass and guide through this journey called life. Especially as you walk in your preordained purpose.

Let the word work! The Bible reassures of this in 2 Timothy 3:17 saying, "God uses it to prepare and equip his people to do every good work." Allow God's word and Spirit to help lead, guide, and fully equip you to do every good work. Give Him the liberty to mold you into the woman that He has predestined you to be. And let the Lord shape you through consistent discipleship, sound doctrine and teaching, and a connection to His word and the body of Christ. Hebrews 10:25 reminds us, "And let us not neglect out meeting together, as some people do, but encourage one another, especially now that the day of his return is drawing near." Jesus is coming back soon, and we've got to be ready from the inside out!

CHAPTER 4

Spiritual Evidence: The Character of an IDENTIFIED Woman

"Until the time came to fulfill his dreams,
the LORD tested Joseph's character."
—PSALM 105:19

D o you remember the story of Joseph in Genesis 37–50? In a nutshell, Joseph was the favored son of Jacob. He was the one whom his father created a coat of many colors for and loved quite dearly. Not only did Joseph receive favor from his natural father, but he also had the favor of God on his life. You see, the Lord gave Joseph a series of dreams that would one day make him second in command to Pharaoh (of course, his brothers didn't like it, but we'll talk more about that part later). Until Joseph's God-ordained calling was to be fulfilled, his character would first need to be tested.

No doubt, Joseph knew who he was, even when it was hard for others to know. He knew his identity. He knew the dreams. He knew what God had placed inside of him. He knew his purpose. But what he didn't know, was what it would cost him to fulfill it.

When God adopts you into the faith and places a dream, vision, or burden inside of you, that's only the beginning. There's so much more that accompanies the calling. Things such as cultivation, experience, training, strength through tests and trials, as well as discipleship and personal discipline (as we discussed in the previous chapter). However, there's something else that goes with it...and that's *character*. It's the proven evidence that you are one of His children. That you are an IDENTIFIED woman.

Let's step away from Joseph for a moment. Imagine a police lineup. In this case, when someone has committed a crime, the victim usually has to identify the individual who has committed the act against them. This is done as the victim pans through all of the faces, carefully, and then pinpoints the perpetrator. It tends to go something like this, "That's the one! That's the one who wronged me!"

And then the police officer asks, "Are you sure?"

The answer, "Yes, officer, I'm sure."

Now, I know (well, I hope), you're not a criminal! But if you are—just in case you're reading this book from a women's prison facility (no judgment here)—this information will help. God accepts you just as you are and is waiting to help you find His purpose for your life. However, my point here with this vivid illustration, is that people should be able to quickly identify you as a Christian. And there should be some evidence. In a crowded room full of people, someone should be able to say, "Yep. That's her! She's the one! She's a Christian."

Your character will identify you. Your servant attitude will identify you. Your integrity will identify you. Your faith will identify you. Your perseverance will identify you. Your reliability will identify you. Also, your joy will identify you.

That's right, joy is another character trait that will prove who you are in Christ. I can recall a time when one of the youth members told a visitor friend of his, "She's the joyful one!" He had no idea that I overheard what he said to his guest, but inside, it made my heart smile. It prompted me to give God glory! And He knew it.

In that moment, the Lord was showing me just how important it is to exemplify a joyful spirit to others. That's character.

People are watching us, sis. People need to see the light of Jesus shining through us. When we have these qualities working in us, they identify us as Jesus' true disciples. It shows that we are His genuine followers. Not only that, but it also glorifies God. Jesus said so in John 15:8, "When you produce much fruit, you are my true disciples. This brings great glory to my Father."

The fruit He's speaking of represents *character*. Galatians 5:22–23 breaks it down this way, "But the fruit of the Spirit is love, joy, peace, longsuffering, gentleness, goodness, faith, meekness, temperance; against such there is no law" (KJ21). There is no law against bearing fruit. Trust me, no one is going to arrest you for showing love to someone. Amen! Quite frankly, the Lord wants us to bear much of it!

Bear much love, much joy, much peace, much patience, much gentleness, much goodness, much faith, much humility, much self-control, and much more other good stuff. Jesus tells us, "When you produce much fruit, you are my true disciples. This brings great glory to my Father" (John 15:8). This is how we are recognized as Christians, sis. And we're not alone, the Holy Spirit will help us. But this is how we show the watching world that we are IDENTIFIED.

THE SPIRITUAL EVIDENCE OF GODLY CHARACTER

We know the world needs Jesus. And you're going to be the one who can point them to Him. But there needs to be some physical evidence, sis. Some evidence that clearly shows that you represent the King of Kings and Lord of Lords. In these last days, the Lord wants you to actively bear witness that you are His. That you are a woman of godly character.

Again, your character—the way you carry yourself, the things you say, how you respond to life's issues and the people around you, and how you live your inner life—will identify you. It will all speak for you. But if your life reflects the world or mirrors the world, then what do you expect the world to say? I'll tell you in one word—*hypocrisy.*

Let's face it. The number one problem that non-believers have with Christians is hypocrisy. They hate it. When the world is looking for a way to escape a life with Jesus, they say, "I don't want to be a Christian if that's what it looks like. They're hypocrites." Ouch! No way! We don't want them to say that about us. We want them to come to Jesus, not run away from Him.

Now, clearly that won't hold weight on Judgment Day. But we, as Christians don't want to be the ones standing in the way of these people making it into heaven someday because of the way we're acting. No. We have a job to do. Jesus tells us, "Go and make disciples," not run them away. That's why we've got to get it together, sis! As Christian women, we have to practice what we preach, live what we believe, and mean what we say. We must respond to our convictions and stand up for what we read in the word of God.

I like the story of Joseph, but I *love* the life of Paul in the Bible, because he was so *bold*! He believed what he said and he proclaimed it. He preached "Christ Jesus!" And it didn't matter what anybody thought of him, he lived to please God. He knew who he was in the Lord and he boasted in that alone. Not only that, but He defended the faith and stood strong through adversity and the persecution that came his way. It was many of Paul's writings (inspired by God) that teach us still to this day, how to *live* the Christian life. And guess what? He did it through the grace of God.

He said in 1 Corinthians 15:10, "But by the grace of God I am what I am, and his grace which was bestowed upon me was not in vain; but I labored more abundantly than they all—yet not I, but the grace of God which was with me" (KJ21). Hallelujah! It's by His grace that we're able to do what we do! I love it!

Personally, I know that I can't do anything without His grace. Whenever I try to do something in my own ability (since we're talking about purpose in this book), it just doesn't come out as good. It's more of a struggle. It just doesn't flow as well. And don't get me wrong, doing God's will is not always easy, but there is definitely a distinct difference when you can sense that you just might be struggling or striving in your own strength or ability. Oh, but when His grace is involved, watch out! Because there's a supernatural flow coming through. It's on!

I need His grace. I need His favor. You need it too. In the NLT, 1 Corinthians 15:10 reads this way, "But whatever I am now, it is all because God poured out His special favor on me—and not without results." Like I said, I NEED His favor. Yet, I also need His results.

My husband's business slogan is "True performance. True results." Meaning, you stay true to what you're supposed to do, and let God take care of the results—He can do it. The Scripture for my husband's company is Philippians 4:13, which proclaims, "I can do all things through Christ who strengthens me" (NKJV). This verse was also one of Paul's writings. Did I tell you that I love Paul? He's one of the men of faith that I really want to meet one day! I sometimes call myself Pauletta! That's my brother, sis. Yep! That's my brother from another mother!

But no, seriously, Paul had a supernatural power working inside of him to please the Lord. And we have that same power, which is the Holy Spirit, working in us. Paul tells us in Philippians 2:12–13, "Work hard to show the results of your salvation, obeying God with deep reverence and fear. For God is working in you, giving you the desire and the power to do what pleases him." God will lead and guide us by His Spirit as we walk out our purpose, just as He led and guided Paul to boldly write, preach, and live the truth.

Paul lived out his Christian life with character, *successfully*. We see that etched throughout his life in Scripture. And God wants to do the same thing with us. We know that in the end, Paul proved to the world, including us today, that he fought the good fight of faith and won! Now, he's awaiting his heavenly prize! That's a win-win situation right there! We have to win in this life, too. But while we're prevailing, let's win some souls for Christ. The Bible tells us in Proverbs 11:30, "The fruit of the righteous is a tree of life, and he that winneth souls is wise" (KJ21). Isn't it awesome how we can find such great wisdom in the book of the Bible that's known for its wisdom?

So let's be wise women and win souls. And let's have godly character while we do it. In the meantime, let's move forward and talk more in detail about becoming this type of woman that will advance the Kingdom of Heaven.

READY FOR THE TEST?

The opening verse of this chapter is Psalm 105:19, which says, "Until the time came to fulfill his dreams, the LORD tested Joseph's character." Usually, before God brings forth His dreams or visions in our lives, we will have to go through some things that prove we are ready to handle the dream or vision that He has given us. In this case, comes the test of character.

The term *character* means a distinctive mark, a figure or symbol used in writing or printing; also a distinctive trait, quality, attribute, characteristic, moral strength, pattern of behavior, personality, or reputation. Your character is similar to your thumbprint. It's what identifies you. And because your identity is in Christ, then your thumbprint should bleed red when you're asked to identify yourself, *figuratively speaking*.

In the natural sense, your fingerprints are what signify that you are who you say you are. Usually in a crime scene, the investigators look for fingerprints as evidence to find or prove which particular individuals committed the crime. They are looking for a distinctive trait. That's what God is looking for with you. He wants to make you distinctive. He's looking for you to stand out. Be different. Be set apart, unique. He also wants you to have qualities, attributes, and characteristics that match His DNA. He wants to prove to the world and those around you that you are indeed His child. That you have been IDENTIFIED.

Are you getting the point here? When God calls you, He has the right to prove you. The real reason is because He wants you to represent Him well. He wants others to experience Him through you. He wants people to know that they can make it through life's tests and trials. Most times, He does this by proving us first, so we can be His living witnesses to His love, goodness, mercy, strength, faithfulness, and power.

I remember when the Lord first called me to go to school to become a teacher, or servant, of the gospel. I knew that He had placed this evangelistic calling on my life to minister to women, but I had no idea what it would take for me to walk in my purpose effectively. My, my, I truly had no earthly idea. Yet, God knew. And He knew that He would be right there with me to carry me through each test and trial, and through the proving process. Have you felt God carrying you, lately? Have you felt God proving you?

Character is proven through tests and trials. It's proven when times get hard or when you're stressed out. It's proven both in the home and outside the home. It's proven with work and assignments that have been given to you, whether at your job or at church. But I have found that the Lord will also use people, especially, to prove us. He did it with Joseph—remember his brothers?

Joseph's brothers hated that God gave him those dreams! I

really don't like using the term "haters," but they were haters! I mean, they despised him so much, that they plotted against him, threw him into a pit, and then sold him into slavery. If that's not hate in action, I don't know what to call it. The Bible calls it like it actually is in Genesis 37:5, "One night Joseph had a dream, and when he told his brothers about it, they hated him more than ever." See what I'm talking about?

Newsflash! Everyone is not going to be as excited about your dreams as you are. But that's okay. When this happens to you, prepare yourself for potential backlash, insults, hurtful words, ugly stares, or jealousy. Prepare to stand strong and take it. Prepare to stand strong in character and do what Ephesians 4:31–32 instructs, "Get rid of all bitterness, rage, anger, harsh words, and slander, as well as all types of evil behavior. Instead, be kind to each other, tenderhearted, forgiving one another, just as God through Christ has forgiven you. So forgive them and do right with the help of the Lord.

Joseph could have lashed out or been mean to his brothers when he became second in command to Pharaoh, but he didn't do that. Sure, he was hurt, but instead, he chose forgiveness. Joseph's brothers didn't have a clue as to why he had been given those dreams. They couldn't understand what God was doing with their little brother. God had chosen Joseph for a special task to help them in the future, during a hard season of famine that was yet to come. Those dreams that they hated so much had a purpose. But before they could be fulfilled, Joseph's character had to first be proven.

Try to embrace the reality that some people are typically not going to understand the dreams, visions, burdens, or passions that the Lord has placed inside of you. They may get it later, or they may never get it at all. Either way, it's okay, sis. Love them and forgive them anyway. Because God has a plan.

I've discovered over the years that He's actually working on both ends of the stick. He's working it all out for the good. In the end, Joseph told his brothers in Genesis 50:20, "You intended to harm me, but God intended it all for good. He brought me to this position, so I could save the lives of many people." Wow! That is a drop the mic moment!

Don't despise God's proving or testing process. He's got a bigger plan for it all. He's trying to save lives and build character in the midst of it. So any test that He allows to happen in your life has a purpose attached to it. Nothing happens by chance with God. He's just testing and proving your faith. He's making you stronger. He's building your endurance.

First Peter 1:6–7 says, "So be truly glad. There is wonderful joy ahead, even though you must endure many trials for a little while. These trials will show that your faith is genuine. It is being tested as fire tests and purifies gold—though your faith is far more precious than mere gold. So when your faith remains strong through many trials, it will bring you much praise and glory and honor on the day when Jesus Christ is revealed to the whole world." Jesus is coming back, sis. So count it all joy when you're tested. You're coming out as gold—shining in exemplary faith and character! While you're glowing, grab a powerful book entitled, *Trials*, by June Hunt. I highly recommend it because the author really breaks down, biblically, what happens in the midst of trials and how God has a unique plan and purpose for them all.

CHARACTER IN EVERYDAY LIFE

Now I'm going to share with you some practical ways of how to walk out godly character in your everyday life. **CAUTION!** Please do not try to attempt any of this without the help of the Holy Spirit. Believe me! I have been there, trying to walk the straight line perfectly, and I just couldn't do it. While we are called to work out our own soul salvation, we are *not* called to work it out alone. God has instilled a supernatural power within us to do it. So here goes...

YOUR CHARACTER AT HOME

I would venture to say, that aside from God, the people in your home know you the best. They live with you. They know when you're happy or angry. They know when you are in balance or all over the place. They know whether you're practicing what you're preaching, or being a hypocrite. They know whether you are loving or unloving. Face it, whether they are your husband, child, mom, dad, sister, or roommate, they know you. They know *us*.

That's why it's important to *practice* living our lives from the inside out. That's actually how my ministry got started. One day, God just placed this burden on my heart to help women all over this world to live a life that pleases and glorifies Him, no matter where we are and no matter who is watching. Christianity is not only about a relationship with Jesus Christ, but it's also about a relationship with others.

God is constantly molding and shaping us to look more and more like His Son. When we are IDENTIFIED and know who we are in Christ, then we can help others become IDENTIFIED and know who they are as well. Then the Kingdom of heaven will just keep growing and growing. That's what this is all about, but it starts with us. And it starts at home.

Now, let me tell you. I know the people who are the closest to us can rub us the wrong way. Trust me. I'm aware of it. But even though we may have arguments or disagreements with those whom we love on the inside, we have to know how to make things right with one another through forgiveness, love, humility, and effective communication. Amen. Most of us would try to make it right with those on the outside, so we have to do the same with those on the inside.

So if you've messed up in the home life area, and I can almost guarantee that most of us have in some way or another (remember my transparent story in a previous chapter?), you simply have to fix it. The key to growth in this area is asking the Lord to forgive you, repenting, apologizing to the one you wronged, and loving deeper. This is what character looks like at home.

Character also starts in the prayer closet. It's like your private sanctuary where you can just talk to God about anything and everything, even as you labor in prayer for others. It starts with personal confession and praying Psalm 51:10, "Create in me a clean heart, O God, and renew a right spirit within me," (KJ21) as often as needed. It starts when you crack open your Bible at the break of day and receive your daily bread. It starts when you love and respect those whom you see first thing in the morning, like your family.

Our inner lives are so important to God and those who live with us. I believe that when we allow God to change us from the inside (our hearts, minds, and actions), then our world on the outside will quite naturally be inspired to change too. Change can be contagious! It can be duplicable. But change starts from within.

As women, we have to live from the inside out! I know that we have a lot of issues going on in our hearts (the Bible tells us so in Proverbs 4:23). I also know that most of our minds are constantly thinking, and we have a built-in tendency to get emotional or anxious at times. Not to mention, we can allow ourselves to become overwhelmed with the demands of our home lives, weekly schedules, and workloads. BUT in all of that, God *still* calls for us to operate in godly character—at home.

He still calls for us to have a repentant heart and to treat those on the inside of our homes with love, respect, and dignity. He also calls us to forgive, show humility, be generous, serve, be patient, be kind, and practice self-control as well. Because the Lord knows if you're loving everybody else on the outside, but not treating those on the inside of your home in these ways, chances are your family is going to be looking at you crossways, saying, "Who is that woman?" *Character starts at home.*

YOUR CHARACTER IN CHURCH

As you see people week after week in your church, and even while working side by side in ministry together, put on love and tenderhearted mercies. Can I say this again? We, as the body of Christ must dwell and work together in love. The Lord instructs us in Colossians 3:14, "Above all, clothe yourselves with love, which binds us all together in perfect harmony." Love binds us together *perfectly.*

I've been in church for many, many years. My grandmother taught me and my younger sister the word of God from a young age, my parents took us to church, and as a young adult, the Lord led me back after my college days. I've been there ever since, by the grace of God. All glory belongs to Him. Amen!

But I say all of this to admit I have had my fair share of tiffs, rips, offenses, misunderstandings, arguments, and hurts in church. I have had my days when it was hard to work side by side with some men and women that I call my brothers and sisters in Christ. It's the truth. Don't get me wrong, we've had a *lot* of great times. However, my point here in my transparency, is that the Lord used those hard and trying moments to mold and shape my character and give me relatable experience. Furthermore, even though those times were definitely tough for me, they were also beneficial in preparing me for my purpose. They not only made me stronger in my faith but also challenged me to a deeper love walk.

Through it all, God taught me how to love beyond offenses. He taught me how to love in spite of wearing my feelings on my shoulder. He taught me how to work well with my brothers and sisters by controlling my own actions. And He definitely helped me to whisper what my refrigerator magnet read, "Lord, keep your arm around my shoulder, and your hand over my mouth!" He really taught me how to genuinely live love in action. And I'm forever grateful for that tough training season.

First John 3:18–20 states, "Dear children, let's not merely say that we love each other; let us show the truth by our actions. Our actions will show that we belong to the truth, so we will be confident when we stand before God. Even if we feel guilty, God is greater than our feelings, and He knows everything." I like that! He's stronger than our feelings. Isn't that a great truth!

God is love. Jesus laid down His life for us—that was love. We are called to love our Christian brothers and sisters. First John 4:20–21 tells us, "If someone says, 'I love God,' but hates a fellow believer, that person is a liar; for if we don't love people we can see, how can we love God, whom we cannot see? And he has given us this command: Those who love God must also love their fellow believers."

So whether your church is small, medium, or large…choose love, tenderhearted mercies, and try to live peaceably among each other if at all possible. Romans 12:18 beckons, "Do all that you can to live in peace with everyone." And I'll join you. Let's show ourselves friendly. Smile. Hug. Fellowship. Serve. Pray for one another. And *love*.

We are reminded in 1 Peter 4:7–8, "The end of the world is coming soon. Therefore, be earnest and disciplined in your prayers. Most important of all, continue to show deep love for each other, for love covers a multitude of sins."

Remember, Jesus tells us in John 13:35, "Your love for one another will prove to the world that you are my disciples." Our love for each other identifies us as true followers of Christ. This is the *evidence* of true, godly character.

YOUR CHARACTER AS A LEADER

Okay, I'm going to talk to women leaders for a brief moment. If God is calling you to lead in any way, shape, form, or fashion—such as teaching a Sunday School class, or leading a women's Bible study, praise team, choir, a business, ministry, or organization—grab a highlighter for this one! Let's talk.

As leaders, we are held to a greater accountability. Especially, as leaders in the church. James 3:1 warns, "Dear brothers and sisters, not many of you should become teachers in the church, for we who teach will be judged more strictly." James gives it to us pretty straightforward here. So this is a pretty serious subject and responsibility. The warning, in its context, is specifically talking about watching our tongues.

What we say and how we treat God's people (and those who may become one of His people) is highly important to the Lord. This is where character needs to be carefully examined. Jesus calls us to be servant leaders. He shows us this in Matthew 20:25–28, "But Jesus called them together and said, 'You know that the rulers in this world lord it over their people, and officials flaunt their authority over those under them. But among you it will be different. Whoever wants to be a leader among you must be your servant, and whoever wants to be first among you must become your slave. For even the Son of Man came not to be served but to serve others and to give his life as a ransom for many."

Jesus was talking to His disciples at that time. And today, He's talking to us. Also, 1 Peter 5:2–4 compliments it saying, "Care for the flock that God has entrusted to you. Watch over it willingly, not grudgingly—not for what you will get out of it, but because you are eager to serve God. Don't lord it over the people assigned to your care, but lead them by your own good example. And when the Great Shepherd appears, you will receive a crown of never-ending glory and honor."

I thank God for discovering the reality and beauty of servant leadership. Naturally, I have a pretty strong personality, and I've worked in corporate, non-profit environments, including the church. And before reading the word of God, I had it wrong! Arrogant, domineering, and dogmatic leadership is not God's way. As Christian leaders, we are called to be humble servant leaders over God's people.

If you struggle in the area of pride, arrogance, or dictatorship in your leadership style, I highly encourage you to grab a few index cards and write out a couple of Scriptures regarding this problem. Begin chiseling away at this destructive, unbiblical, and ineffective behavior before you fall miserably, stain your character, or even ruin your reputation. It's not worth it.

There is nothing like seeing a Christian leader, whether in the church, in the music industry, or on the big stage step down from their platform with bad character or full of pride. It just stinks. It's a bad witness to the life of faith. The world, once again, sees it as hypocrisy. Ephesians 5:15–17 tells us, "So be careful how you live. Don't live like fools, but like those who are wise. Make the most of every opportunity in these evil days. Don't act thoughtlessly, but understand what the Lord wants you to do."

He wants you to be a servant leader. A good book that I recommend on this subject is entitled, *God's Secret to Greatness: The Power of the Towel*, by David Cape and Tommy Tenney. Another good book that is specifically designed for women in leadership is *Servant Leadership: A Biblical Study for Becoming a Christlike Leader*, by Rhonda H. Kelley. And one more that I want to share with you is called *Leadership...Biblically Speaking: The Power of Principle-Based Leadership*, by David Cottrell.

I hope and pray that this is helping you as a leader or an upcoming leader. Just remember that the Holy Spirit will help you. You are not alone in the process. Don't expect to be perfect. Just follow His lead, and be a servant leader. Joseph was a servant leader, and Jesus was the ultimate example of servant leadership when He got down and washed His disciples' feet. He showed them, and us, how it's done. We can do this!

Allow me to share just a few helpful, practical suggestions of what servant leadership can look like in everyday life. As a leader, you not only serve through teaching or leading on a particular project or assignment, but you also care. Ask if the individuals under your leadership need help with anything. Listen to their concerns, ideas, or suggestions as well as your own, and give them some consideration. Pray for them. Take them out to lunch, buy breakfast, or purchase a gift simply to show your appreciation. Say words like, "Thank you." Tell them, "I appreciate all of your help," or "You did a great job!" Encouragement goes a long way. This is what it looks like in reality.

It's all about treating those who have been entrusted to us, or whom we influence, well. Don't forget, one day we want to hear, "Well done, thou good and faithful servant" (Matthew 25:21 KJ21). So let's continue to do good, remain faithful, and serve God's people well.

EVIDENCE REVEALED

Look back in your own life and see if there are traces or evidence of wholesome godly character in your life. How are you faring in this department? It's always good to do a self-examination. Paul tells us in 2 Corinthians 13:5, "Examine yourselves to see if your faith is genuine. Test yourselves." As I mentioned earlier, oftentimes, before God uses us greatly with dreams or visions, our character will be proven and tested. We saw this with Joseph and we are not exempt.

Your love walk will be tested. Your morals will be tested. Your leadership will be tested. Your inner life will be tested. Your endurance will be tested. And your integrity will be tested.

Remember, Joseph's integrity was tested when Potiphar's wife attempted to seduce him and then lied about it. He could've compromised his loyalty to God, but instead, he fought her off and stayed faithful to the One who called him.

That's what the Lord is looking for in our lives. Faithfulness in character and in living our lives worthy of the calling. Remember what our great brother Paul tells us in Ephesians 4:1–3, "Therefore I, a prisoner for serving the Lord, beg you to lead a life worthy of your calling, for you have been called by God. Always be humble and gentle. Be patient with each other, making allowance for each other's faults because of your love. Make every effort to keep yourselves united in the Spirit, binding yourselves together with peace."

Joseph endured all the hardships, stood strong through the lies, took the extra jail time, and forgave his brothers for selling him and hurting him the way that they did. His character was tested and it was proven. He passed the test and the Lord fulfilled His purpose for his life.

Proven godly character goes along with our purpose, sis. It's a package deal. We don't want to be women who possess wonderful gifts, but lack good, moral character. Instead, we want to be women who have been proven to be found faithful and who remain connected to the Vine, which is Jesus Christ. May I remind you, when we do this, we will produce much fruit. This brings our Father great glory!

PART TWO:

Moving Forward in Your Purpose

"The Lord will fulfill his purpose for me; your steadfast love, O Lord, endures forever. Do not forsake the work of your hands."
—Psalm 138:8 (ESV)

CHAPTER 5

*Spiritual Courage: Laying
Aside Doubt, Insecurities,
Comparison, and Fear*

"This is my command—be strong and courageous!
Do not be afraid or discouraged. For the LORD
your God is with you wherever you go."
—JOSHUA 1:9

This is God's command to you, as well. When God calls you, just as He did with Joshua and so many others in the Bible, He equips, prepares, and gives a word or command to move forward. Realistically speaking, when it's time to move forward into your purpose, oftentimes there is a little apprehension. It's the fear of the unknown, uncertainty, failure, inadequacy, and the looming thoughts of what others will think or say. These are all considered natural feelings or emotions, but when He calls you, He will take care of all of that!

He's actually doing it right now. He's showing you at this very moment, as you read this book, that He will be with you. He tells you so in His word at the very opening of this chapter. The question is, do you believe it? Answering that question will be the defining moment for you. Because it will take spiritual courage to step out and walk in His divine purpose for your life.

Let me pause here for a brief moment before we move on. I want to remind you that when God begins to unravel your purpose, it will unfold little by little, and day by day. Along the way, He will give you noticeable signs, confirmations, glimpses of His presence, and speak to you loudly through His word and through others with sound, biblical advice or encouragement. It will be a supernatural process of revelation regarding His will for your life. Have you experienced any of what I'm talking about?

Again, God's will gradually unfolds. In a natural sense, it's like cutting the skin off of an apple or peeling an orange. There are layers of training and preparation, and time is necessary to grow in experience. But through this process, you'll become relatable to others in your field and to those who need to know how to walk this Christian life *effectively*. Think about it. When that skin of the apple or peel of the orange is removed and cleansed, it's ready to be eaten!

That's the way it is with purpose. When it's time, you'll be ready for people to eat off of your plate of life, and you'll be prepared to give them what God has given you to feed them (sort of like the story of Joseph). In the word, 2 Timothy 2:21 says, "If you keep yourself pure, you will be a special utensil for honorable use. Your life will be clean, and you will be ready for the Master to use you for every good work."

God has been preparing you and making you ready for every good work. He's been spiritually equipping you in so many ways. Ways that you are aware of, and probably ways that are still unbeknownst to you. Nonetheless, He's been priming you to walk courageously in your calling. Before I talk more about spiritual courage, I want to share with you a personal experience of being strong and courageous.

Normally, when I'm out and about, particularly when I'm going out to eat or walking in the shopping mall, I keep little encouraging

Scripture cards in my wallet. They cost about fifteen cents each, and I purchase them regularly from Christian bookstores such as Family Christian, Lifeway, or Mardel's (stores that I love and frequently shop). What I do, is have them handy, just in case the Holy Spirit prompts me to give someone a card. One card reads, "God knows your purpose—Do you?" And it has Jeremiah 29:11 inscribed on it, "'For I know the plans I have for you,' says the LORD. 'They are plans for good and not for disaster, to give you a future and a hope.'"

Now, this is a card that I use when I'm talking to someone about their purpose. I specifically recall a time when I was on a mini getaway with my hubby Calvin in Houston, Texas. I was simply shopping through some racks of clothing. Then all of a sudden, the Holy Spirit nudged me gently and wanted me to spark up a conversation with the store clerk. I was like, "Lord, really, now? What do I say to her? How do I start the conversation?" Talk about having to follow the command of, "Be strong and courageous!"

When I approached this young lady at the register and asked about her purpose, she was very intrigued by the question. She began to open up to me about what she was studying in school and looking to do with her life. Granted, it had nothing to do with the Lord, but it was an open door of opportunity for me to ask her about *God's* purpose for her life. She paused and said, "You know, I don't know." At that moment, the Lord filled my mouth to speak a word in due season to her.

Proverbs 15:23 says, "A man hath joy by the answer of his mouth: and a word spoken in due season, how good is it!" (KJV). And oh, how good it was! We really had a wonderful conversation. The Lord used that opportunity for me to plant a seed of doing *His* will for her life. I pray that she will discover her purpose in life and hopefully, I'll see her on golden streets one day with many souls accredited to her account!

I've learned over the years that once you step out in faith and obedience, the Lord will fill your mouth to give you the right words to say and lead you to do what He wants you to do. I'm reminded of the prophet Isaiah. In Isaiah 50:4, he states, "The Sovereign LORD has given me his words of wisdom, so that I know how to comfort the weary. Morning by morning he wakens me and opens my understanding to his will."

That's what this life is all about. It's about doing His will. Jesus came so that we could have abundant life on earth, but He also came to show us by example how to be true disciples and witnesses to the life of faith. He wants us to invite others to experience and enjoy a relationship with Him, but He also wants us to encourage others to walk out their callings and purposes too. Selfish or worldly ambitions simply won't make the cut. And I believe that's why the Spirit of God prompted me to talk to this young lady at that very moment.

Jesus speaks directly to this point in Matthew 16:24–26, "Then Jesus said to his disciples, 'If any of you wants to be my follower, you must give up your own way, take up your cross, and follow me. If you try to hang on to your life, you will lose it. But if you give up your life for my sake, you will save it. And what do you benefit if you gain the whole world but lose your own soul?'" Selfish ambition is not worth it. Gaining the world's approval over God's approval is not worth it. Doing your own thing is not worth it. But doing God's will and walking in His purpose it worth it all!

Jesus tells us this in Matthew 7:21, "Not everyone who calls out to me, 'Lord, Lord!' will enter the Kingdom of Heaven. Only those who actually do the will of my Father in heaven will enter." As you digest this verse, I want to clarify that yes, we *can* work in the secular environment and still do what God has called us to do. I've been there. Today, there are many Christians working in the corporate sector or service industry who are nurses, doctors, attorneys, and leaders in the marketplace who love the Lord, and pray for and witness to those around them.

God can use us for His glory anywhere. The important thing is to make sure that we're fulfilling His will and purpose for our lives wherever He desires. Anything else would be laboring in vain. And we certainly don't want to do that. We're called to do *His* will when, where, and how He wants it done. And when we do it this way, our labor is *not* in vain. First Corinthians 15:58 reassures, "So, my dear brothers and sisters, be strong and immovable. Always work enthusiastically for the Lord, for you know that nothing you do for the Lord is ever useless." Amen!

Time is running out. We have to do God's will. That's why we're talking about this right now in this book and in this season. We have work to do, sis. It's time to not only do what we're called to do, but also help others do the same. Trust me, I know it can be scary witnessing to others whom you don't know from Adam. I get it. Actually, one of the little fifteen cent cards that I've carried around with me reads, "It's scary out there." But then the word inscribed on it states, "But when I am afraid, I will put my trust in you" (Psalm 56:3). Trust in Him, sis.

Once you have been IDENTIFIED in Christ, know your God-given gifts and calling, and are constantly preparing through ongoing discipleship and personal discipline (while also developing character in the midst of it all), then it's time to press on and move forward into what God has purposed you to do, and encourage others to be IDENTIFIED as well. This will not only take strength and courage, but it will also require you to lay aside any doubt, insecurities, comparisons, and fear as you gird up to move forward in faith.

LAYING ASIDE DOUBT

When you begin to step out in faith towards walking in your purpose, sometimes doubt will begin to rear its ugly head. Yep!

There is no doubt about it! That's why you have to make a conscious effort to lay it aside.

The term *doubt,* by definition, means to feel uncertain about or be afraid of; it's a feeling of uncertainty, hesitation, and unsureness. It brings on confusion. Not only that, but if not careful, entertained doubt could very well cause you to run away from God's will or not move when He says to move. In God's eyes, it's actually sin and that's why when doubt strikes, we have to strip off this weight.

Hebrews 12:1 warns about this, "Therefore, since we are surrounded by such a huge crowd of witnesses to the life of faith, let us strip off every weight that slows us down, especially the sin that so easily trips us up. And let us run with endurance the race God has set before us." Doubt is a weight that will slow you down. It will trip you up. It can also cause you to waver in your faith.

Unfortunately, doubt has the tendency to cause us to waver and question God's supernatural plans and direct answers for our lives. For example, when you and I pray and ask God for wisdom, the Bible tells us in James 1:5, "He will give it to you. He will not rebuke you for asking." James 1:6–7 goes on to say, "But when you ask, you must believe and not doubt, because the one who doubts is like a wave of the sea, blown and tossed by the wind. That person should not expect to receive anything from the Lord. Such a person is double-minded and unstable in all they do" (NIV). Ouch! Don't waver. Don't doubt.

God is telling you right here that if you ask Him what you should do in anything, when He answers, receive it by faith, and don't doubt His divine provision. He has answered. The word of God just explained this. However, Satan would love for you to doubt the answers or direction that God has given you. I know all about it.

The enemy knows that doubt is the direct opposite of walking by faith. That's why we have to watch out for his sneaky implantations of doubt. Furthermore, we have to purposefully uproot it and replace it with seeds of faith. Quite frankly, we actually have more power over doubt than we know! When we replace doubt with faith, it gives us the power to tear down, uproot, and move mountains. Jesus states in Luke 17:6, "If you had faith even as small as a mustard seed, you could say to this mulberry tree, 'May you be uprooted and be planted in the sea,' and it would obey you!" This is Jesus talking to His disciples. You are a disciple, sis.

All it takes is a mustard seed of faith. Have you ever seen a real mustard seed? It's a very tiny seed. Jesus is saying here that that's all you need. All you need is a little bit of faith to uproot and move mountains in your life! So what is the mountain that's standing in your way right now? What's holding you back from doing all that God has called you to do? Is anyone around you planting seeds of doubt in your mind? Are you wavering with the answers of God? Are you allowing doubt to crowd out the truth?

Don't let it! Uproot it! Speak to the mountain. Speak the word of God in faith and believe. Hang up encouraging words to help you believe. I've had to put the word of God regarding faith over doubt all around me in one season of my life.

That was a time when doubtful thoughts were really strong and nearly overwhelming me. But it was no one but God, reminding me to believe Him over everything and everyone that spoke against or above His word. I love the bold words of Paul in Galatians 1:10 where he proclaims, "Obviously, I'm not trying to win the approval of people, but of God. If pleasing people were my goal, I would not be Christ's servant." I love Paul. As a servant of Christ, he stood strongly for the truth of God's word above all else. We should follow his example, humbly.

The Bible tells us in Hebrews 11:6, "But without faith it is impossible to please him. For he that cometh to God must believe that he is, and that he is a rewarder of those who diligently seek him" (KJ21). So don't waver, just believe. This type of faith pleases God and launches you forward! It's time to lay aside any doubt.

REPLACING INSECURITIES WITH A GOD CONFIDENCE

Take this moment to identify any insecurities in your life right now. Are there any? Is there anything that you can pinpoint that you may be insecure about? Is it your looks, weight, home life, kids, marriage, position, social status, your talents, or even your *lack* of confidence?

I want to tell you that as an ambassador of Christ, you don't have to walk with your head held down, in shame, or guilt. You are a child of God! Now, don't get me wrong. If there are some things that you need to work on that may be causing some of these insecurities, meaning things that can be fixed, then go for it. But don't beat yourself up over it. God wouldn't want you to do that. Needless to say, the type of insecurities that I'm talking about here are specific to your purpose. And the key to replacing insecurities and accomplishing this type of God confidence will be dependent upon your wholehearted *trust* in Him.

Jeremiah 17:7 states, "But blessed are those who trust in the LORD and have made the LORD their hope and confidence." This is a very powerful Scripture when you believe it. Do you see the emphasis stressed here on "the Lord?" Put your trust in the Lord. Make the Lord your hope and confidence. Are you grasping this?

Building your confidence starts with the word of God. The word will be so crucial and highly beneficial when you are stepping out in faith to walk in your purpose. No doubt, there will be times when you may feel insecure or wonder if a particular move is a God-directed move or decision? But when you put your trust, hope, and confidence in the Lord, REJOICE, because He promises that He will never fail you or forsake you.

Remember, the Lord spoke in Joshua 1:9, "Be strong and courageous! Do not be afraid or discouraged. For the LORD your God will be with you wherever you go." In this passage of Scripture, He's telling you through His word not to be discouraged, to know that the Lord your God will be with you everywhere. This is a call to believe. This is a call to build your confidence, and to know that you can take Him at His word. God has a proven track record.

You are not reading this book by chance. I have prayed for women who will pick this up, order it, download it, or listen to it on audio. I believe that this is a timely message for women across the globe to take their places and walk in their God-given purposes with a God confidence.

And I'll tell you, the more you spend time in God's word, the more your confidence will grow! Then it won't matter what people say, think, or feel, or what the enemy places in your mind, because you will have placed your trust, hope, and confidence *in the Lord*. He's got your back. Not only that, but when you do this, the Bible says that you are blessed! That means you are highly favored. So, look out for that supernatural favor when God calls you to move forward in your purpose. From experience, I know it to be true, and it is *awesome*!

So whatever negative perception you may have about yourself, let it go. Whatever insecurities you have, let them go. Begin to think positively and encourage yourself in the Lord like King David did (see 1 Samuel 30:6). By the way, the next time you look into the mirror say to yourself, "I trust God. I have placed my hope and confidence in the Lord. I am a child of God. I have been adopted into the faith. He knows my name. I am loved by Him. I am IDENTIFIED."

Declaring these words of affirmation and the promises of God over your life will boost your confidence in no time! Believe the word. Believe that God is with you and for you, and not against you. He wants the best for you. So place your faith in Him, speak life over yourself, and while you're at it, consider grabbing these additional resources by Wendy Treat, *Take a God Look at Yourself*, and Joyce Meyer's book, *The Confident Woman*. Within these books, I think you'll find amazing treasures that speak directly to this particular subject. I admit, I'm only scratching the surface.

I pray that what I've shared with you will help give you just a little more confidence as you move forward in your purpose. I also pray that you'll shake off any insecurities and replace them with a God confidence. You are a child of God. He's got you, sis. Just trust Him.

THE GAME OF COMPARISON

Can I say that there is only one you? Well, it's true! There is only one you. So embrace this beautiful reality. You are different. You are unique. You are you. So don't waste your time or energy by rivaling against others or by playing the nasty game of comparison.

God made you special and for a special task. So playing the devious game of comparison will only chip away at your God confidence. It will make you feel inadequate, incapable, or defeated. Plus, it's a joy-killer. Not only that, but it demolishes motivation and productivity. And it's ungodly no matter how you slice it up.

If you begin comparing yourself to others and don't catch it at the starting point, it will only open the door for the enemy to bring in sins such as jealousy, envy, malicious behavior, slander, quarreling, and strife. And you don't want that. You don't want that negative baggage weighing you down as you're trying to do the will of God. The key to ending this senseless game is realizing that it's actually happening, and then renewing your mind with the word of God, so that you can quickly overcome it. I'm speaking from experience because I've been there.

In the past, I've played the comparison game. I've had the self-pitying thoughts of, "Lord, why isn't it happening for me?" Or, "I don't have as many Twitter followers or Facebook *likes* as this one or that one does." It's sheer foolishness, right? I'm being transparent here.

One day, my husband had to tell me, "STOP! Stop comparing yourself to others. Be who God has called you to be. Don't worry about other people's numbers. Just do what you do and be the best at what you do." I love my husband! He was right. I really had to come to the reality and say, "Wait! You're right. I can only reach whom God has called me to reach. And it's okay."

This renewed mindset changed my outlook in this area. It not only helped me to rejoice over what God was doing in other people's lives and ministries but also allowed me to praise the Lord for what He was doing in my own life and ministry, too. Romans 12:15 tells us, "Be happy with those who are happy." This mindset helped me to ride in my own lane, drive at God's pace for me, and go hard at what He has preordained me to do. I encourage you to do the same. Ride in your own lane. Go at the pace God has set for you. And go hard at what He has preordained you to do. Don't forget to rejoice when others are rejoicing. *This* is God's way.

Listen. You are very valuable to the Kingdom of God. The body of Christ needs you to be you. Everybody has a part to play. Just like Paul and Apollos. One watered and one planted, but God ultimately brought forth the increase (see 1 Corinthians 3:1–8). And guess what? According to 1 Corinthians 3:8, "both will be rewarded for their own hard work." Take pleasure in the fact that God will reward you for your hard work, sis. Just be the best *you* that you can be and fight the urge to play the game of comparison.

CHOOSING FAITH OVER FEAR

When God calls you to a specific task, assignment, or calling, sometimes what He's asking you to do might seem a little scary or challenging. It might take you out of your comfort zone and move you away from your norm. It could take you to a place where you've never gone or envisioned yourself ever going before. It might even cause you to question whether you can actually do it. Yet, that is when you'll have to make the conscious effort to choose faith over fear.

Many people in the Bible, whom God called to do some amazing things, had to make this choice. Moses was one, and Joshua was another one. There was also Gideon. Now Gideon has an interesting true story. There are some golden spiritual nuggets within Gideon's calling. The Bible tells us in Judges 6:12, "The angel of the LORD appeared to him and said, 'Mighty hero, the LORD is with you!'" Of course, he didn't feel like a mighty hero at the time. Gideon's people were being defeated by the Midianites (their enemies), yet God had allowed it for seven years because of the Israelites rebellion against Him. But at that moment, and after hearing the prayers of His people, God was calling Gideon to step up to the plate to end the attacks against Israel.

God said to him, "Go with the strength you have, and rescue Israel from the Midianites. I am sending you!" (Judges 6:14). Wow! Look at that calling! But even though God had called him, Gideon wanted to make sure that the Lord was going to be with him, because the Midianites' army was huge! So he asked for a sign. To make a long story short, God confirmed that He was *indeed* going to be with him as he stepped out to do what He was calling him to do (see Judges 6:33–40).

The lesson in this part of the story is that it's okay to ask the Lord to confirm His will for your life *before* you make a move. Because you want to be sure that before you make a major decision, it's really from God, and that He is going to go ahead of you and be with you. But once He confirms it to you in His own special and supernatural way, then move. Do what He says and trust that He will be with you, just as He was with Moses, Joshua, and Gideon.

In a nutshell, after God told Gideon to go rescue His people and everything was confirmed, the Lord wanted him to cut his numbers down tremendously. There were too many people with Gideon to fight this particular battle. And guess who couldn't go with him to help win the battle? Are you ready? The fearful. Yep! The Lord said, "Whoever is timid or afraid may leave this mountain and go home." There were 22,000 of them who chose to go home (see Judges 7:3). They were afraid. It was a choice.

Please don't allow fear to stop you from answering the call of God. Please don't let fear hinder you from moving forward in your purpose or following through on something that God wants you to do. Trust me. I know all about fear, and how it can try to paralyze you from pressing onward to do what God is calling you to do. But Gideon's real life story of the Bible helps me to stand my ground and choose faith over fear.

In the end, God trimmed Gideon's army down even further at the stream, and he was left with only 300 warriors! God told him, "With these 300 men, I will rescue you and give you victory over the Midianites. Send all the others home" (Judges 7:7). Wow! We serve a MIGHTY and BIG God! He is a Warrior!

By faith, trust, and God's amazing power, they won! God gave them the victory by having them blow rams horns while breaking clay jars and holding blazing torches in their hands, shouting at the top of their lungs, "A sword for the LORD and for Gideon!" (see Judges 7:19–20). Talk about a supernatural victory! That's how they defeated the Midianites. God provided and stood firm on His word that He would be with Gideon.

That's what we have to do, sis. We have to stand firm on God's word. He's faithful. When I had to make a major decision in my life concerning God's purpose for me, no doubt I was afraid. It was overwhelming fear. Yet, I kept hearing the Holy Spirit whisper to me, "Trust God." I also saw and heard a lot of, "Walk by faith and not by sight." The word *faith* was all around me. He kept telling me, "Nothing is impossible with God." I saw it almost everywhere. He was answering prayers and giving me signs galore. I fasted, prayed, sought godly counsel, and everything! At the height of it all, all signs pointed to, "Be strong and courageous! Do not be afraid or discouraged. For the LORD your God will be with you wherever you go" (Joshua 1:9).

The word "go" stood out to me. The words, "do not be afraid" increased my faith. And "I will be with you wherever you go" gave me courage. The Bible tells us in Psalm 119:105, "Thy word is a lamp unto my feet, and a light unto my path" (KJ21). The word lit up my path. It got to a point where I literally took my Bible, put it on the floor, and stood on top of it, declaring that I was going to stand on what His word was saying to me no matter what. And I did!

Sis, no matter where you are, what you may be facing right now, or what decisions you need to make, when God calls you to step out in faith—follow Him. Choose faith over fear. Let the word light your path. And fight the deception from the enemy to go against what you know God has shown you in the Bible and through His confirmations and guidance.

I know choosing faith over fear is not easy. However, once you hold your fearful thoughts or apprehension to the word of God and stand on it, fear will diminish. But it's an active choice that only you can make.

Here are a few Scriptures that I want to share with you that I hope and pray will help you in choosing faith over fear. Before I share them, here are some quick suggestions. It would be great to post some of these verses around your house, at work, in your home office, or store them in your phone. This will help remind you of what God's word says when the enemy throws darts of doubt your way. We'll talk more about how to protect and guard yourself against him in the next chapter. But for now, here are the Scriptures that I promised...

"For God hath not given us the spirit of fear, but of power and of love and of a sound mind."
—2 Timothy 1:7 (KJ21)

"Don't be afraid, for I am with you. Don't be discouraged, for I am your God. I will strengthen you and help you. I will hold you up with my victorious right hand."
—Isaiah 41:10

"I lay down and slept, yet I woke up in safety, for the Lord was watching over me. I am not afraid of ten thousand enemies who surround me on every side."
—Psalm 3:5-6

"But when I am afraid, I will put my trust in you."
—Psalm 56:3

"Trust in the Lord with all your heart; do not depend on your own understanding. Seek his will in all you do, and he will show you which path to take."
—Proverbs 3:5-6

"For we walk by faith, not by sight."
—2 Corinthians 5:7 (KJ21)

"I sought the Lord, and He heard me, and delivered me from all my fears."
—Psalm 34:4 (KJ21)

"So be strong and courageous! Do not be afraid and do not panic before them. For the Lord your God will personally go ahead of you. He will neither fail you nor abandon you."
—Deuteronomy 31:6

He will be with you wherever you go as you move forward in your purpose. I can testify to that!

CHAPTER 6

Spiritual Warfare: Get Ready for Battle

"Therefore, put on every piece of God's armor so you
will be able to resist the enemy in the time of evil. Then
after the battle you will still be standing firm."
—EPHESIANS 6:13

Okay, it's time to gird up, my sister. Because once you say *yes* to do God's will, then it's on! You enter into what's called "spiritual warfare." That's right! And Satan will be on your trail. However, this is nothing to be afraid of. We've already covered choosing faith over fear, so don't worry. Instead, as you walk out your purpose, this will be the time to *be* strong and courageous. But it will also be the time to put on the full armor of God and be ready for battle.

Anytime you're about to do something big in your life, especially when it comes down to doing God's will, our great enemy Satan will NOT be excited about it. He'll actually try to figure out how he's going to strategize against you. He'll work on smoothly crafted schemes to try and stop you from accomplishing your mission successfully. But don't be too alarmed, because the Lord will prepare you and fully equip you to fight back and win.

When I began writing this book, I knew that I was going to experience spiritual warfare. God had already begun preparing me for it. Everything around me related to, "Put on the full armor of God." There was an upcoming class at church about it, books all around me on the subject, and I'd even bought a coffee mug with the verse on it that was already in my kitchen cabinet. So when I opened the door to the cabinet in this particular season, that mug was staring me right in the face, warning me to get ready for battle.

Once I saw all of these promptings of God around me, I decided to go to the Christian bookstore to purchase a plaque that I'd previously seen that read, "Therefore, put on the full armor of God, so that when the day of evil comes, you may be able to stand your ground" (NIV). That is God's word! That is Ephesians 6:13! And it is so true. Those very words were preparation words for upcoming spiritual attacks. Even as I write (at this moment), I have that plaque sitting right next to my laptop. It's a constant reminder for me to put on the full armor of God.

I'll tell you, I'm in the trenches. I'm *in* the battle. There is no qualm about it. The enemy doesn't want me to get this information to you. But it's okay. I'm up for the challenge! Because God has already prepared me to recognize the enemy's presence, realize that I'm not wrestling against flesh and blood, to be sober and alert, and to stay vigilant in the overall process.

When it comes down to spiritual warfare, the great thing is that we're not alone. God's got our backs! And the word of God is alive and powerful! On top of these facts, the enemy is waging war against IDENTIFIED warriors for Christ!

My sister, you are a warrior woman! You are IDENTIFIED. Own your new title, and get ready to take your position and stand your ground. Because it's time to get ready for battle. God is telling you right now to "put on every piece of His armor." In this way, you'll be protected against the onslaught of the enemy's attacks.

You've got work to do and souls to win. You've got people to reach, lives to influence, and a calling on your life that only you can fulfill. So in this chapter, you're going to learn how to put on every piece of God's armor, recognize spiritual warfare when it's upon you, resist the devil when he comes to tempt you, and stand firm against his evil schemes as you do what God has commissioned you to do in this season and beyond. It's time to get dressed.

GETTING DRESSED FOR THE INVISIBLE BATTLE

In Ephesians 6, the Apostle Paul teaches us about how to get dressed for the battle. He lets us know that we're *not* fighting against flesh and blood (people), but that it's a spiritual war. He alerts us in Ephesians 6:12 telling us, "For we are not fighting against flesh-and-blood enemies, but against evil rulers and authorities of the unseen world, against mighty powers in this dark world, and against evil spirits in the heavenly places." It's an invisible battle!

As we press to accomplish God's purposes for our lives as wives, moms, single women, ministry leaders, church or community volunteers, students, entrepreneurs, corporate executives, authors, and bloggers, we have to make sure that as we are doing what we've been placed on this earth to do, we are spiritually armed and ready for an enemy attack. We must be protected as we guard our hearts, minds, homes, and purposes against the enemy's fiery darts and schemes.

Right now, I'm going to show you how to be fully dressed from a biblical and practical perspective as you get ready to engage in spiritual warfare and win! Follow me as I break down the belt of truth, breastplate of righteousness, shoes of peace, shield of faith, helmet of salvation, sword of the Spirit, and the importance of consistent prayer (see Ephesians 6:14–18).

THE BELT OF TRUTH

Ephesians 6:14 says, "Stand your ground, putting on the belt of truth." The first piece of God's armor that you will need to put on is the belt of truth. To give you a little background knowledge about the purpose of the belt, I'm going to give you a brief synopsis of why it's so important to strap on this piece of armor first.

In the time the Bible was written, the Roman legionaries (soldiers), put on the belt initially. The reason why is because they needed to tie up anything that was loose, so there wouldn't be any unnecessary distractions as they fought the enemy. The belt was a great way to take care of this potential issue. All they had to do was tuck away anything that was hanging outside of their gear, so that they wouldn't get sidetracked during the battle.

Let's take it to the present day for us as it relates to spiritual warfare. When we gird up with the belt of truth, meaning our obedience to God's word, while upholding integrity and being pure in our hearts, minds, and actions, then we can fight effectively against the enemy's coming attacks. On the contrary, when lies, deceit, immorality, hypocrisy, or lack of obedience to God's word is blatantly obvious, watch out! Because if those things are hanging out in our lives, and not taken care of quickly and moved out of the way, then we leave ourselves open for an enemy attack.

Those hanging issues are huge distractions and sinful. The enemy knows it. As long as that stuff is running loose in our lives, he's going to try to use it against us. Think about it. How many leaders and Christian households have we watched fall prey to this? It's real. So put on your belt of truth. Because without that belt, things will just be all over the place and cause you to be non-effective as you try to walk out your purpose.

Here's a quick look from a natural perspective. If you don't have a belt on your jeans or pants, quite naturally, that's going to feel pretty uncomfortable. At least, it's uncomfortable for me! My point here is that before you walk out of the house, something should immediately prompt you to say, "Whoa! I forgot my belt!" Because if you don't have that belt on, most likely it's going to be a distraction for you the rest of the day (and other people might notice it too).

Well, it's the same way spiritually. When we don't gird up with the belt of truth, we leave the door open for unnecessary distractions and room for the enemy to take notice. That's why it's so important to stay focused and be a woman of truth. Remember, you've already been IDENTIFIED as a God-fearing child of the Lord. So if there is anything hanging around in your life that should not be there, take care of it by girding up your loins with the belt of truth so that you can fight effectively and without all of those unnecessary distractions in the way.

THE BREASTPLATE OF RIGHTEOUSNESS

Moving onto the second piece of God's armor. Ephesians 6:14 says, "Stand your ground putting on...the body armor of God's righteousness." This is the part of the armor that protects your chest. In regards to spiritual warfare, it means protecting *your heart*. As a righteous woman of God, you have to guard your heart with everything within you, every fiber of your being. Proverbs 4:23 says, "Guard your heart above all else, for it determines the course of your life."

The King James Version puts it this way, "Keep thy heart with all diligence; for out of it are the issues of life." That "it" is referring to your heart. Jesus speaks concerning the heart through Matthew 15:19, "For from the heart come evil thoughts, murder, adultery, all sexual immorality, theft, lying, and slander." All of this stems from the heart. And all of these are considered the issues of life.

Of course there are many issues of life. Issues such as unforgiveness, bitterness, anger, envy, depression, criticism, impurity, ungratefulness, temptation, and the list could go on.

These are the inner struggles that nobody else can see. This is the stuff that Jesus warns us that we need to get rid of in our lives. In Matthew 23:28 He says, "Outwardly you look like righteous people, but inwardly your hearts are filled with hypocrisy and lawlessness." Jesus is talking about the inner life of people who proclaim to be followers of God. So let's not be like the religious Pharisees. Instead, let's live righteously from the inside out—from the heart.

A good Scripture that helps us keep our hearts clean before the Lord, and as we do His will is actually the theme verse for my ministry. It's Psalm 51:10 which says, "Create in me a clean heart, O God, and renew a right spirit within me" (KJ21). This Scripture works! I actually have it on my refrigerator as a reminder to keep my heart pure before Him. But here's a quick practical nugget for you. Whenever you're dealing with something in your life that you know is not of God, bring it to His throne room of grace, and ask Him to cleanse your heart and renew a right spirit within you. He's faithful to do it.

One more thing about guarding your heart. Colossians 3:14 tells us, "Above all, clothe yourselves with love, which binds us all together in perfect harmony." Love comes from the heart, and the enemy is the total opposite of that. Love binds the body of Christ together. So guard your heart with all diligence. Don't let the enemy pierce it. Instead, be on guard and love God, love your family, love those whom you serve, and love your neighbor as you love yourself. Keep in mind, love is another attribute that identifies you as Jesus' true disciple. And it's also a weapon that can used against the enemy.

My sister, remember you are a child of the Most High God. Living in His righteousness will not only classify you as an IDENTIFIED woman, but it will also make the enemy take ten steps back as you do what God has called you to do. So stay dressed, stay clean, and stay guarded.

THE PREPARATION OF THE GOSPEL
(KNOWN AS THE SHOES OF PEACE)

Ephesians 6:15 explains, "For shoes, put on the peace that comes from the Good News so that you will be fully prepared." In this Christian life, as you walk in God's righteousness and proclaim the gospel message to others, expect that there will be a spiritual fight. The fight may come as a sickness, a tough trial, internal conflict (at home or with those closest to you), or simply immense pressure that you know could only be spiritual warfare. Knowing this will help you prepare yourself to stand strong when these things strike your life. This is the time when you will need to rely on God's supernatural peace.

In biblical times, before battle, the Roman soldiers had to make sure that their feet were properly covered as they prepared to fight. They put on heavy-soled military sandals studded with tough nails underneath so they would be able to handle any rough terrain that could potentially hinder their progress. The sandals also had leather straps that were wrapped around their calves to aid in keeping them tightly in place. These were their war shoes!

For you, this part of the armor is all about being ready to share the gospel wherever you go, while standing your ground against the enemy as you do it. God will give you the strength and He will also give you peace that will sustain you. Psalm 29:11 says, "The LORD gives his people strength. The LORD blesses them with peace."

Here's another one for the road ahead. Psalm 18:39 proclaims, "For thou hast girded me with strength for battle; Thou hast subdued under me those that rose up against me" (KJ21). God is in the fight with you, sis. Your job is to prepare yourself to stand strong in the evil day, while having done all to stand. May the peace of God be with you as you move forward in your purpose. Stand strong and stand your ground.

SHIELD OF FAITH

Ephesians 6:16 instructs, "In addition to all of these, hold up the shield of faith to stop the fiery arrows of the devil." When doubt, unbelief, or fear comes to attack your mind or stifle your progress, put up the shield of faith. Pick it up and protect yourself. Speak the word over your life and situation. It's amazing how when you activate your faith, the doubt, fear, insecurity, and skepticism will all have to cease.

You have the power to stop the fiery darts from reaching you. The Bible confirms this in Isaiah 54:17, "No weapon that is formed against thee shall prosper; and every tongue that shall rise against thee in judgment thou shalt condemn. This is the heritage of the servants of the LORD, and their righteousness is of me" (KJ21). This is your heritage as an IDENTIFIED woman in Christ. And God has girded you up with spiritual armor that will help quench the fiery darts from succeeding against you.

Sometimes you might have to physically raise up your arm to motion that you are not going to allow the enemy or his attacks to prosper or stop you from moving forward in what God has preordained you to do. I've had to do that before. It was a time when I forgot all about this spiritual weaponry. I was so tired and worn out, that I felt like I didn't have anything left in me to fight. Have you ever been there before?

Yet, in the midst of my fatigue, all of a sudden, the Holy Spirit whispered to me, "Pick up your shield of faith." It was so clear. So I did it. I actively motioned picking up an imaginary shield and holding it up in front of me. That simple act of obedience actually strengthened my faith, and I was able to move on.

Faith in motion is a powerful thing! And the enemy knows it. Keep in mind, we're fighting an invisible battle here. So cover yourself by trusting God at all costs, and make sure to take Him at His word. Quench the devil's fiery darts today by holding up your shield of faith.

THE HELMET OF SALVATION

Ephesians 6:17 tells us, "Put on salvation as your helmet." When I think about this piece of armor, I tend to say to myself, "I am saved. So I need to think like a saved woman." Salvation is all about deliverance. Once we accept Christ, we are IDENTIFIED in Him. But remember, that's just the beginning.

In Romans 12:2, Paul reminds us, "Don't copy the behavior and customs of this world, but let God transform you into a new person by changing the way you think. Then you will learn to know God's will for you, which is good and pleasing and perfect." The enemy knows that when you start changing your life and attitude according to God's word, that's when the Lord will start unfolding His will for your life. That's when Satan knows that he's got a fight on his hands.

All the more, that's why you need to keep your helmet on. It will protect you. It will serve as a protective garment from the devil's infiltration of negative or evil thoughts that could later turn into detrimental actions. Sin not only stems from the heart but it also comes from the mind.

With this foreknowledge, guard your mind by casting down toxic thoughts that you know are against what God's word says. If you're thinking negatively about people or letting life's circumstances weigh you down in your thought life, check it. Those thoughts are just unnecessary weights. Instead, release them, renew your mind with God's word, and let the Holy Spirit keep you from falling into sin.

Another suggestion would be to find Scriptures regarding those particular thoughts to counteract it. Philippians 4:8 tells us, "Fix your thoughts on what is true, and honorable, and right, and pure, and lovely, and admirable. Think about things that are excellent and worthy of praise." This is what the helmet of salvation does for us. It helps us to keep our minds fixated on the right things—things that are pleasing to God. Remember, salvation is all about deliverance. So stay free and think like a saved woman. Keep your mind protected, so you can do the will of God with a clear head.

THE SWORD OF THE SPIRIT

This is the word of God. I just heard Bibleman! I'm sorry, that's my mama verbiage coming out. We have so many *Bibleman* movies for my kiddos that it's etched in my brain. But that's a *great* thing! I personally, LOVE the word of God. It's my roadmap for my life, and it helps me to live out my purpose with power.

So that's what we're going to talk about next—your weapon. The sword of the Spirit is a weapon, and it CUTS! Ephesians 6:17 tells us about this last piece of armor. It says, "And take the sword of the Spirit, which is the word of God." This is the piece of weaponry that you *fight* with.

No matter what you face in this life, the word of God will be your best defense. When the enemy comes towards you with his evil tactics and schemes against you, take up your sword and cut him. This is the only time you can be violent and be okay with God! But seriously, the way to defeat the enemy is to prepare yourself by reading the Bible, studying it, memorizing Scriptures, meditating on what you've read, and speaking the word out loud. It will not only give you power, but victory!

Stay in the word of God, sis. It will be your greatest weapon against the enemy in the time of spiritual warfare. Use it skillfully and with power. Pick up your sword and fight!

PRAYER

I can't stress enough how important having a consistent prayer life is, my sister. The Bible tells us to "pray without ceasing" (1 Thessalonians 5:17 KJ21). That means to keep praying. In other words, don't stop praying. I talked about this in an earlier chapter.

When we pray and bring our petitions to the Father about others and ourselves, that's a weapon against the enemy within itself. Honestly, Satan can't stand it when we pray. If he could stop us every time, he would. But he can't. Thanks to God! Yet, that doesn't stop him from trying.

I have a few questions for you. What will do you to fight the enemy as it relates to your prayer life? How will you fight off his barrage of distractions? How will you stand your ground in this area? Because you've got to stand firm in prayer as you do what God is calling you do.

There is no way that I could do what I do, without prayer. I pray anywhere, anytime. I pray in the car or while I'm doing my hair and getting ready to go somewhere. I pray while I'm washing dishes, cooking, ironing, and sweeping the kitchen floor (I especially like this time of prayer). I pray as I'm folding clothes, also while I'm waiting for a meeting to start. I pray over my meals. And I especially pray before, during, and after doing something for the Lord (e.g., ministry work). Lastly, I pray before I counsel, give advice, or witness to someone.

Are you getting the point? I pray without ceasing. I pray about nearly everything. Philippians 4:6–7 says, "Don't worry about anything; instead pray about everything. Tell God what you need, and thank him for all he has done. Then you will experience God's peace, which exceeds anything we can understand. His peace will guard your hearts and minds as you live in Christ Jesus." I have a beautiful plaque on my living room coffee table that reads, "Thank God for what you have. Trust God for what you need."

Prayer is a lifestyle. It's our lifeline and connection to God. It's how we communicate to our Father in this spiritual life. And it's crucial when fighting the enemy. There is a lot of power in prayer.

Why do you think there are so many books written about it? Pray, my sister. Stay connected to God, and win! Now that we know what to wear in this spiritual battle, let's take a closer look at how to recognize it when it's coming.

HOW TO RECOGNIZE SPIRITUAL WARFARE

In this segment, since I'm also a blogger, I'm going to share an excerpt from one of my blog posts on this actual topic. In this particular post, I discuss how to *recognize* spiritual warfare. I think this is significant because if we don't know the signs of the attack, then we could be caught unaware. And we don't want that! So here goes...

If you are a Christian, guess what? You are going to experience spiritual warfare. Yep! And now that you know, that's only half the battle. The next step is recognizing how to deal with it, when it strikes!

Whether you believe it or not, we do have a real enemy. Actually, the moment you get out of bed to move forward in faith, your next assignment, a new level, or your destiny, Satan will be right there to wage war against you, because he hates progress. He doesn't want to see you grow further in your walk with Christ, help other people, trust God deeper, or fulfill your purpose.

And now that you know this, what are you going to do about it? *Pause and consider.* I hope you said, "Fight!" If so, that's exactly right! Fight on your knees in prayer. Fight by pressing deeper into God's word. Fight by moving forward in faith in spite of the opposition or distractions. And fight by responding properly when your emotions are out of whack.

YES! As women, we have to learn this one! When we are busy doing things for our family, home life, work, ministry, or personal spiritual growth, Satan will definitely try to cause problems by using our emotions to get us to sin against God. He will also do this to try to kill our witness. He knows that when we are emotionally high, that is prime time to get us to act out of character or make foolish decisions. Not to mention when the pressure is on!

So be sensitive to your emotions, but also when you feel immense pressure, LOOK OUT! *Recognize what's happening, because you could be entering into spiritual warfare.* Pay attention to what's occurring in your life and examine yourself. Are you advancing the Kingdom of God? Are you active in your church? Are you helping your pastor succeed? Are you stepping out in faith for something? Are you taking time to pray more for your family or others? Are you reading more of the Bible? Are you trusting God more? Are you stepping out into new territory? Is God opening new doors for you? All of these things can bring on a spiritual attack.

Yet, if any of these are happening, the key to standing strong through it is recognizing where you are and fighting. You can't win a spiritual battle with fleshly weaponry. The Bible speaks of this in 2 Corinthians 10:3–4, "We are human, but we don't wage war as humans do. We use God's mighty weapons, not worldly weapons, to knock down the strongholds of human reasoning and to destroy false arguments."

The reality is that you can't win in spiritual warfare by having a bad attitude, complaining, losing your temper, throwing things, talking crazy to people, withholding affection, holding a grudge against people, or giving people the silent treatment. That is not godly. Ephesians 6:12 says, "For we wrestle not against flesh and blood, but against principalities, against powers, against the rulers of the darkness of this world, against spiritual wickedness in high places" (KJ21). *So don't fight people, because they are not the real enemy.* Whatever you do, recognize the spiritual attack and win the battle!

That's my blog! I pray that this post just ministered to you. I tend to say, "It's all about real life, real talk, and real faith." I believe God called me to create this blog to inspire, encourage, and speak truth about real life issues that we deal with as Christian women today. In saying that, feel absolutely free to check out my blog that comes out every Monday at 7:30 a.m. at www. insideoutwithcourtnaye.org. It's all about letting God change us from the *Inside Out* before Jesus comes back! Ok, enough of the commercial break, let's talk about how to resist the enemy and stand strong against his schemes.

RESISTING THE DEVIL AND STANDING FIRM AGAINST HIS SCHEMES

In order to resist the enemy, I think we need to take a deeper look into what that actually looks like in real life. To *resist* means to oppose, fend off, fight back, argue, or work against. It is also defined as refusing to cooperate or yield, and to stand firm against something. Now look at this in the sense of resisting the devil and standing firm against his schemes.

As you move forward in your purpose, you are going to have to resist him and be aware of his cunning and strategic plots against you. Because whether you can sense it or not, he is plotting. Simply because he does not want you to accomplish God's plan for your life. Furthermore, he does not want you to be effective while doing it. That's why you're going to have to gird up while watching and standing firm against his tactics.

Watching his schemes is all about staying sober and alert. The Bible informs us in 1 Peter 5:8–9, "Be self-controlled and alert. Your enemy the devil prowls around like a roaring lion looking for someone to devour. Resist him, standing firm in the faith" (NIV). Many women reading this verse may say, "Yep, I know this one! I've heard this Scripture before." Truly, ladies, that's great! But *knowing* this verse is simply not enough. It's time to *act* on it.

Your power, defense, and victory will depend upon your application of God's word, *not* just reading it or knowing it. James 1:22 warns us of this saying, "But be ye doers of the word and not hearers only, deceiving your own selves" (KJ21). Without biblical application and self-control, the devil doesn't have to deceive you, you'll do it to yourself. So while knowledge is great, application is what will bring the victory!

Resisting the enemy's schemes and temptations is all about saying a strong, "NO!" It's saying no to his sneaky temptations, promptings, distractions, and sinful delights. I say delights, because he makes things look good. You know it! He makes that nasty movie or music video look good. He makes that guy at the office or church, who is NOT your husband or fiancée look good. He even makes having fun instead of grinding on a deadline look good.

But, NO! We've got to stay focused and self-controlled. Those deceitful delights are just strategically crafted schemes and distractions that the enemy uses to try to throw us off course and get us out of sync with the Holy Spirit. But don't give in to it! Instead, stand firm against his wicked strategies and keep moving forward in your purpose.

Fight, sis. Resist him with God's supernatural strength and holy word. The Bible tells us in James 4:7, "Submit yourselves therefore to God. Resist the devil, and he will flee from you." When we submit to God's word, we then have the power that we need to resist the enemy. And the Bible tells us that he will then flee from us. So believe this truth and press on! Don't get hung up with Satan's foolishness. Keep working and get the job done successfully.

Listen, as you do God's will, expect spiritual warfare. Expect the enemy to use people to get you thrown in a tizzy or distracted from what needs to be accomplished. Keep your eyes open for his cunning tactics and watch out for your own flesh. Quite frankly, we don't have time to be ensnared by Satan's crafty traps or lured away by our own lusts or deceptions right now.

Instead, we need to stay fully dressed for battle and girded up with God's full armor on. We must recognize that we *are* in a spiritual war, and realize that we have the power to resist the enemy and his schemes, as we stand strong together in our faith in these evil days. It's time to win! It's time to fight the right way. The Kingdom of heaven is at hand. Let's gird up!

CHAPTER 7

Spiritual Empowerment: Unleashing the Holy Spirit Power within You

"But you will receive power when the Holy Spirit
comes upon you. And you will be my witnesses, telling
people about me everywhere—in Jerusalem, throughout
Judea, in Samaria, and to the ends of the earth."
—ACTS 1:8

About a year ago (at the time of this writing), I went to a
conference in Plano, TX and the leader of that prophetic
conference, Irvin Baxter of Endtime Ministries, Inc., boldly
declared, "We're living in a time like the book of Acts!" When
I heard those words, it put a fresh fire within me! I knew God
was in the building, giving that message to put a new charge in
me to spread the gospel—everywhere! We are living in a time,
my sister when we have to unleash the Holy Spirit power that
we have inside of us as IDENTIFIED women of Christ, and move
forward to advance the Kingdom of Heaven! The early apostles
did it, and so can we!

The world needs Jesus Christ! Would you agree? Too many
people are losing sight of who they are on a natural level, but we
are also seeing this happen within the body of Christ (the church).
This is *not* the time to be losing sight of our identity. Instead, it's

time to know who we are in Christ, so that we can confidently and boldly move forward in our purposes.

Unfortunately, many churches on a global level have begun to get a little too comfortable, complacent, and lackadaisical. The term *lackadaisical* means lacking enthusiasm and determination; being lethargic, passionless, spiritless, lazy, careless, and sluggish. Yikes! On the other hand, the early church of Acts was on fire for God, seeing miracles take place and experiencing thousands come to salvation!

Peter, the apostles, and Paul took the world by storm! They knew the power they had within them, and went forth boldly proclaiming the gospel message to the world around them. As a result, thousands were saved. If we are going to make a thumbprint in the world for Jesus Christ, then we have got to get recharged!

Paul told young Timothy, "I charge thee therefore before God, and the Lord Jesus Christ, who shall judge the quick and the dead at his appearing and his kingdom: preach the word; be instant in season and out of season; reprove, rebuke, exhort with all longsuffering and doctrine" (2 Timothy 4:1–2 KJ21). In this passage of Scripture, Paul was preparing Timothy to walk boldly in his calling and to gird up for the Great Commission. God was using Paul to equip him to go forth in his purpose. And that was to preach the Good News. But in the next passage, he also warned him about a time that was coming.

Paul told him in 2 Timothy 4:3–4, "For a time is coming when people will no longer listen to sound and wholesome teaching. They will follow their own desires and will look for teachers who will tell them whatever their itching ears want to hear. They will reject the truth and chase after myths." But this is what Paul tells Timothy in verse 5, "But you should keep a clear mind in every situation. Don't be afraid of suffering for the Lord. Work at telling others the Good News, and fully carry out the ministry God has given you."

I pray that this puts a fresh new fire within you to proclaim the Good News. This message is for you! Keep a clear mind. Don't be afraid of suffering for the Lord. Fear not, as the Scriptures declare. Work at telling others the Good News. And fully carry out the ministry—the purpose that God has given you.

Whatever God has called you to do, at the end of the day, the ultimate purpose is to lead others to know Christ. That purpose may be demonstrated through living your godly life as a Christian, speaking it, witnessing to others about it, preaching it, writing it, or any other way that God calls you to do it. The point here is that you were created to be a born-again believer, and to share the gospel however and with whomever the Spirit of God leads you.

Again, we are running out of time to do this, my sister. It's time for the church to rise up and proclaim the Good News as the early church did in the book of Acts. They were empowered by the Holy Spirit and they went forth with supernatural power and boldness to bring forth healing, miracles, and deliverance. They accomplished this with the power that was within them. I don't know about you, but I am ready to boldly proclaim the Good News in these last days.

THE POWER OF ACTS THEN AND NOW

In the book of Acts, Peter and the apostles preached the Good News without fear. In the opening verse Acts 1:8, Jesus declares these words to the apostles, "But you will receive power when the Holy Spirit comes upon you. And you will be my witnesses, telling people about me everywhere—in Jerusalem, throughout Judea, in Samaria, and to the ends of the earth." That message is for us today, as well. Once we have accepted Jesus Christ as our Lord and Savior, we receive the promised gift of the Holy Spirit. He is our inheritance too!

In Ephesians 1:13, Paul tells us, "And now you Gentiles have also heard the truth, the Good News that God saves you. And when you believed in Christ, he identified you as his own by giving you the Holy Spirit, whom he promised long ago." As born-again believers in Christ, we are IDENTIFIED through the promise and power of the Holy Spirit. With this knowledge and empowerment, you can turn this world upside down for Jesus!

Peter, Paul, the other apostles, and many others spread the Good News throughout the Mediterranean and beyond! They were empowered and they shared the message of Jesus Christ, His death, burial, resurrection, and atonement everywhere. *Now let me ask you this question.* Who has God placed in your life to share the Good News with? Have you been spreading the gospel message and the word of your testimony with others, lately?

The hour is getting late. And you and I are called to be a part of the Great Commission. We are called to "go and make disciples," as Jesus proclaimed in Matthew 28:18–20. It reads, "Jesus came and told his disciples, 'I have been given all authority in heaven and on earth. Therefore, go and make disciples of all the nations, baptizing them in the name of the Father and the Son and the Holy Spirit.'" And this is what Jesus goes on to say, "Teach these new disciples to obey all the commands I have given you. And be sure of this: I am with you always, even to the end of the age."

He was speaking even unto the end of the world. He will be with us as we fulfill this Great Commission. We are those *new* disciples. And Jesus is telling us to do the same thing. Go and make disciples. It's about Kingdom advancement. It's about unleashing the power that is within us before Jesus returns.

HOW TO UNLEASH THE SPIRITUAL POWER WITHIN US

The Holy Spirit is the power within you. You have it. In other words, He will lead you to those who need to know and accept Christ as their Lord and Savior. But here are a few biblical and practical ways of how to unleash the spiritual power that is within you.

Pray and ask the Lord to give you the Holy Spirit boldness and confidence to proclaim the message of Jesus Christ to those He leads you to. When you encounter them, talk about His birth, time on earth, death, resurrection, and blood sacrifice for our sins (His atonement). And as the Spirit leads you, share your personal testimony of how you were saved and what salvation means for you today.

The Bible tells us in 1 Peter 3:15–16, "And if someone asks about your hope as a believer, always be ready to explain it. But do this in a gentle and respectful way. Keep your conscience clear. Then if people speak against you, they will be ashamed when they see what a good life you live because you belong to Christ." In other words, when you share your testimony or the Good News with others, do it respectfully. Don't try to shove it down their throats or shout it in ALL CAPS on Facebook or Twitter. Use wisdom, follow what Scripture says, and be sensitive to the Holy Spirit.

Also be ready to give a word in due season. You do this by preparing yourself through a devoted time of Bible reading and study, memorizing Scripture, meditating on what you've read and learned, and praying. Also, surround yourself with good Bible teachers at your local church. Another practical method is to research additional resources that will help you share Christ, effectively.

Then, when the time comes for you to share your faith with a lost, dying, hurting, confused, or unidentified world, you'll be ready. You'll be ready to help deliver them from a life of sin and to receive Christ and the Holy Spirit. Furthermore, you'll also be ready to encourage another believer in Christ when the Holy Spirit leads you to help him or her as well. That's unleashing the power that is within you.

So whether you're at the mall, grocery store, airport, restaurant, ballgame, doctor's office, coffee shop, or in line at a register, be ready to share your faith. Be instant in season and out of season. Meaning, be ready at all times when the Holy Spirit quickens you to speak up. Also, be ready to encourage another believer at church, Bible study, a women's conference, worship concert, work, or wherever you find yourself in the company of another fellow disciple. We're in this together. So just step out in faith and let God use you.

The Holy Spirit will give you the words that you need to say. Just ask Him to fill your mouth with the truth and go forth in His boldness. Jesus tells us in John 14:17, "He is the Holy Spirit, who leads into all truth." He is our Advocate. He is our Guide. He is our Comforter. And He is our Helper. We need Him as we witness to others about Christ. His supernatural wisdom will empower you.

THIS GOSPEL CANNOT BE HINDERED

You, or this message, cannot be hindered! In Peter and Paul's day, the gospel message could not be hindered. God saw to it that the truth about Jesus Christ would not be stopped—no matter who tried to prevent it from going forth.

Look at this biblical truth. In the book of Acts, we see that the high priest and his officials, who were the Sadducees, were filled with jealousy because Peter and the apostles were spreading the gospel about Jesus, healing the sick, casting out demons, and saving thousands of people. So they conspired against them and threw Peter and John into jail. Well, guess what happened?

The Bible tells us in Acts 5:19, "But an angel of the Lord came at night, opened the gates of the jail, and brought them out. Then he told them, 'Go to the Temple and give the people this message of life!'" Hallelujah! The gospel cannot be hindered!

Look at what it also says in Acts 5:21, "So at daybreak the apostles entered the Temple, as they were told, and immediately began teaching." Wow! Look at the power of God and their obedience! Now, once the priest and the officials got word that the apostles were somehow released, someone went to them shouting, "The men you put in jail are standing in the Temple, teaching the people!" (Acts 5:25). I love it! Didn't I tell you, the gospel cannot be hindered!

Now this is the part that you really need to see and grasp. They arrested the apostles *again* and brought them before their high council where the high priest confronted them saying, "'We gave you strict orders never again to teach in this man's name!' he said. 'Instead, you have filled all Jerusalem with your teaching about him, and you want to make us responsible for his death!'" (Acts 5:28).

So this was Peter and the apostles' bold response to him in Acts 5:29–32, "We must obey God rather than any human authority. The God of our ancestors raised Jesus from the dead after you killed him by hanging him on a cross. Then God put him in the place of honor at his right hand as Prince and Savior. He did this so the people of Israel would repent of their sins and be forgiven. We are witnesses of these things and so is the Holy Spirit, who is given by God to those who obey him." Looks like the *truth* to me!

For clarity purposes, let me say this. Don't misinterpret this passage of Scripture. Because it is *not* telling us that we shouldn't obey human authority, and neither am I. There are too many verses that instruct us to obey wise counsel and instruction given through leadership. However, what Peter is showing us is that when it comes down to the uncompromising, unwavering, clear word of God, whether people agree with us or not, we *must* follow God and His word rather than man. We must follow truth at all costs.

The purpose of godly leadership across the globe is to teach, equip, and encourage us to do what God has called us to do. Anything short of that is laboring against the truth. Ephesians

4:11–12 says, "Now these are the gifts Christ gave to the church: the apostles, the prophets, the evangelists, and the pastors and teachers. Their responsibility is to equip God's people to do his work and build up the church, the body of Christ."

If those religious leaders the apostles faced would have said, "How can we help you preach this Good News with the power God has given you?" That would've been great! But they didn't. Instead, they were jealous and couldn't allow themselves to be excited about the inner strength, calling, and power that Jesus had given His disciples, so in return, they brought opposition. They tried to hinder the message instead of helping it to go forth. Nevertheless, God set the apostles free to do what He had called them to do—unhindered.

The key here is to not let anyone or anything stop you from speaking or proclaiming the truth of God's word or spreading the gospel of Jesus Christ in whatever way God calls you to do it. What Peter and the early apostles went through was nothing shy of opposition. Yet, they let God fight their battles as they stood their ground for truth, and in the end the Lord delivered them. If they would've listened to the religious leaders and obeyed them *over* God, they would not have reached thousands for the gospel's sake. So be bold, stand strong for truth, and proclaim the Good News as the Spirit of God leads you, just as they did in the book of Acts.

I need to say something here. If you are a woman in any form of leadership, help the people whom God has entrusted under your care to do what *He* has called them to do. Let God use you to teach, equip, and encourage them. Also, serve them humbly, respectfully, willingly, jointly, and enthusiastically. If this is your position, lead well and lead by the Book. We're all working together to populate heaven with the power of the Holy Spirit. Let's do this—*unhindered*!

IS SPEAKING IN TONGUES FOR TODAY?

The answer is a clear and unwavering, "Yes." Regardless of how some people may feel about it, according to God's word, it is for New Testament believers, today. So let's talk about this extra power that God bestows upon those who ask for it.

Before we get started, I need to say that unfortunately, this is a topic that causes much controversy in the body of Christ. I say unfortunately, because it holds so much power in helping to do God's will, such as building up the church, fighting against the enemy's spiritual attacks, interceding for others, and gaining personal strength. So for a moment, let's talk about it.

In the book of Acts, the Day of Pentecost was actually the first account of the apostles and many others, regarding speaking with other tongues. Acts 2:2–3 recounts, "Suddenly, there was a sound from heaven like the roaring of a mighty windstorm, and it filled the house where they were sitting. Then, what looked like flames or tongues of fire appeared and settled on each of them. And everyone present was filled with the Holy Spirit and began speaking in other languages, as the Holy Spirit gave them this ability." *This roaring sound that came from heaven and the powerful description of what looked like flames or tongues of fire represented God's supernatural presence among all who stayed to receive His gift of the Holy Ghost power—120 believers in total!*

Peter had to let everyone else who witnessed this powerful experience know that there was absolutely nothing wrong with those who had received this new heavenly language and power. In fact, he boldly stood before the crowd and declared these words to them in Acts 2:17–18, "'In the last days,' God says, 'I will pour out my Spirit upon all people. Your sons and daughters will prophesy. Your young men will see visions, and your old men will dream dreams. In those days I will pour out my Spirit even on my servants—men and women alike—and they will prophesy.'"

We are living in the last days. And speaking in tongues is definitely for today. I need to mention here that speaking in tongues is *not* about being charismatic, over-emotional, or crazy. It's not about what denomination anyone claims or what church we fellowship in. And it's totally not about us. Instead, it's all about God's presence, His word, and His supernatural empowerment to change lives through His Spirit. So I believe that we really need to be careful not to arrest the Spirit, put Him in a box, or quench Him because of our beautifully crafted programs, events, or fears due to lack of knowledge or personal belief.

Instead, we need to read the word of God and allow the Holy Spirit to interject our church services, prayer meetings, conferences, concerts, and lives, by letting Him have His way. I believe that if we do this around the globe, then we *will* see true revival and lives changed for the better. Personally, I think it's high time for the body of Christ as a whole to come together on one accord in the Spirit to win thousands of souls to Christ again. Just as we saw in the book of Acts!

Now, let me clarify a few things through the word of God. The Apostle Paul asked in 1 Corinthians 12:30, "Do we all have the ability to speak in unknown languages? Do we all have the ability to interpret unknown languages? Of course not!" Paul was speaking about public gifts of tongues and interpretation, not private tongues (which is to build yourself up when you're weak or need to intercede for others). Pray for wisdom and understanding here.

Paul clearly tells us in 1 Corinthians 14:4, "A person who speaks in tongues is strengthened personally, but one who speaks a word of prophecy strengthens the entire church." So you see here that there is a unique difference in tongues, but I'm not going to go too deep into this (I covered the gifts of tongues in a previous chapter). But just so you know, there's personal tongues and public tongues.

Personally, my experience with speaking in tongues is for personal strength and edification. The first time I ever spoke in tongues was at the age of twelve. There was the laying on of hands and when that happened, I *did* actually experience the power of the Holy Ghost with the evidence of speaking in tongues. Paul talks about the laying on of hands in Acts 19:6. It reads, "Then when Paul laid his hands on them, the Holy Spirit came on them, and they spoke in other tongues, and prophesied." *Prophesied* in this context means to edify, exhort, and comfort.

I have to admit that when I first experienced it, I didn't speak in tongues for a while, because I wasn't in a church that practiced or encouraged it. However, later, the Lord led me to a new church in my young adult married life, and for over thirteen years, it has become a part of my personal prayer life. So for personal edification, I do pray in tongues to be strengthened.

Furthermore, if I have a dream about something or someone— that's also when I can intercede in my heavenly language. Praying in tongues is just a great way to pray for people's needs, even when we don't know exactly what's going on in their individual lives. It's also a great way to pray when we don't have answers in our own lives. It's so awesome, because the Holy Spirit knows exactly what's going on and that's when *He* can quicken us to pray according to God's will.

The Bible confirms this truth when it says, "And the Holy Spirit helps us in our weakness. For example, we don't know what God wants us to pray for. But the Holy Spirit prays for us with groanings that cannot be expressed in words. And the Father who knows all hearts knows what the Spirit is saying, for the Spirit pleads for us believers in harmony with God's own will" (Romans 8:26–27). So there you have it. Speaking in tongues is actually pretty awesome and very powerful!

If I could describe it creatively, I would say that it's like prayer on steroids! It just gives you that extra supernatural boost. It has the power to give you that additional charge and boldness as you do what God has called you to do. So even though as believers, we all have the Holy Spirit living inside of us to lead and guide us through our daily lives, but the power of the Holy Ghost (i.e. the evidence of speaking in tongues) just gives added strength and edification to the body of Christ.

Now, let me tell you how NOT to use it. Whether you have the gift of tongues, interpretation of tongues, or tongues for personal edification, speaking in tongues is *not* an everyday language that you use as you are talking to people in a normal conversation. That's when people will think you are crazy. The sole purpose for speaking in any tongue is to build up the church, build up your inner man (or woman), and allow the Holy Spirit to intercede and work in a supernatural way (beyond you and others), while also showing God's amazing presence and power to the unbeliever. Yet, no matter how it's done in any case, Paul warns in 1 Corinthian 14:40, "But be sure that everything is done properly and in order" (NLT).

If you're reading this right now and have any of these gifts or have experienced the power of the Holy Ghost with the evidence of speaking in tongues, I encourage you to continue using it (or them) wisely and as often as the Spirit leads you. However, if you have never experienced praying in the Spirit, you can pray and ask the Lord for it. Ultimately, He knows exactly what you need.

But note here, whatever you do, if don't have it, please don't feel bad about it, don't condemn yourself, and certainly, don't scoff at it or forbid it (see 1 Thessalonians 5:20 and 1 Corinthians 14:39). Also, don't be afraid of it. I believe *fear* might be the culprit or reason why there's been so much controversy over God's word about it.

One more thing that I *need* to say here before I close this section is this, God's presence can come anytime or anywhere He wants. He knows what setting and what environment is prime for a Holy visitation and who is ready to receive Him in this supernatural way. The power of His Spirit can happen in a regular church service, concert, prayer meeting, conference, or even in your home during private prayer.

Whenever, wherever, or however it happens, embrace the moment. It's His supernatural presence. And it's not something that happens in every meeting, event, or prayer time, but when it does occur, bask in it and give Him glory!

To bring this all together, the gift of tongues, interpretation of tongues, and speaking in tongues for personal edification (i.e., building up and strengthening your inner-man) is available to us today. I don't know about you, but I welcome the outpouring of His Spirit with open arms. I desire all that God wants to offer unto me that will make my witness and ministering to others more effective for building His Kingdom.

For further understanding of speaking in tongues, pray and ask the Lord to lead you in His word and allow His precious Holy Spirit to give you revelation, knowledge, wisdom, and more understanding on the subject. Also, a book that I recommend is *The Holy Spirit* by John Bevere. He gives a thorough Scriptural context of understanding who He is, His purpose, and His power. Grab it!

MOVING FORWARD WITH POWER

When I look back and read the book of Acts, I am astounded at the amount of souls that were saved during that time. I just know that *we* can do it again by the empowerment of God's Spirit. We've heard of waves of salvation with Bible greats such as Billy Graham and his amazing life-changing crusades, the Spirit-empowered Azusa Now Revival (by TheCall), and so many others like them.

But what about the church leaders, pastors, prophets, evangelists, apostles, and teachers today? What about you and me?

In these last days, the Lord said He will pour out His Spirit on men and women alike and He will do miraculous things through us. He will show forth His power, deliverance, and glory through us. He will do this with the empowerment of His Holy Spirit. It's through the power of the Holy Spirit that individuals are saved from death to life and in Jesus' name.

Listen. You and I are simply the vessels and the temples that house Him. So when it's time for someone to be saved, healed, and set free, the Spirit of God will be unleashed to transform their lives forever! I hope you're ready to be used mightily for God's glory in these last days. Because you and I have been chosen for such a time as this!

I want to echo God's word to you. My sister, you are a royal priest! You are a living stone! You are God's very own possession! You are IDENTIFIED through His Spirit. Ephesians 1:13 says, "And when you believed in Christ, he identified you as his own by giving you the Holy Spirit, whom he promised long ago."

First Peter 2:5 and 9 also declares, "And you are living stones that God is building into his spiritual temple. What's more, you are His holy priests. Through the mediation of Jesus Christ, you offer spiritual sacrifices that please God—for you are a chosen people. You are royal priests, a holy nation, God's very own possession. As a result, you can show others the goodness of God, for He called you out of darkness into His wonderful light."

Jesus is the light of the world, and because He lives within you, through His precious Holy Spirit, you can be salt and light on this earth. It's time to shine bright, my sister. Jesus is coming back soon. Let's do our part and get ready to save countless souls before He returns. It's time to move forward and unleash the power that is within us!

CHAPTER 8

Spiritual Movement:
Occupy Until He Comes

"And he called his ten servants and delivered them ten
pounds, and said unto them, 'Occupy till I come.'"
—Luke 19:13 KJV

It's time to MOVE! After all that we've talked about, let me
ask you again, what has God called you to do? What is your
purpose? Have you discovered your gifts? Have you discovered
your calling? What talents do you have to invest into Kingdom
advancement? Because as an IDENTIFIED woman, Jesus is telling
you, "Occupy until I come."

If you don't know your purpose yet, don't beat yourself up over
it, God knows exactly what you've been placed on this earth to do.
I believe that He will show it to you. I'll join you in prayer on it.
But in the meantime, do what you know to do. If you're a mother,
be the best mom you can be. If you're a nurse, be the best caretaker
you can be. If you're an entrepreneur, be the best business owner
you can be! The angle here is to be the best at whatever you're doing
right now, wherever you're doing it. Yet, as you do, shine bright and
share Jesus!

Let God use you right where you are. And if He wants
you to do more, He's faithful to show you. But the point here

is to use your gifts, talents, and abilities that He has given you to advance the Kingdom of heaven by sharing His Son with whomever you can influence today. He wants you to occupy until He comes.

That's what the opening parable is all about. It's about not burying your talents, but using well what Jesus has given you to spread the Good News before He comes back. Look at what it says in Luke 19:12–13, "He said therefore, A certain nobleman went into a far country to receive for himself a kingdom, and to return. And he called his ten servants, and delivered them ten pounds, and said unto them, Occupy till I come" (KJV). In this parable Jesus is talking about a nobleman, but in reality, He's speaking about Himself and us. In other words, He's showing His servants that yes, He would have to go away for some time, but when He returns, He will be looking to see how we invested our time and talents.

Jesus is coming back soon, which means swiftly. And when He comes, you won't have a minute more to try to make up for lost time or unused talents. It will be too late for excuses! Also, when He comes back, He will be coming with rewards and judgment, so please use well what has been given to you. His word confirms this in Matthew 25:29–30, "To those who use well what they are given, even more will be given, and they will have an abundance. But from those who do nothing, even what little they have will be taken away. Now throw this useless servant into outer darkness, where there will be weeping and gnashing of teeth."

Listen. It's all about occupying with the supernatural power of the Holy Spirit that is within you, until Jesus comes! God never intended for you to sit on your hands in church or in this world and do nothing. Being an IDENTIFIED woman is all about truly knowing who you are in Christ, growing in your walk with the

Lord, and being fully equipped to move forward in your purpose. Jesus has called you to unleash the power that is within you, go and make disciples, be fishers of men, be an ambassador for Him, and occupy until He comes.

In this book, I've covered a lot of things with the supernatural power of the Holy Spirit working within me. The Lord placed this message on my heart and commissioned me to write it to you (I'm occupying until He comes). With that being said, it was written to encourage you to be all that God created you to be before Jesus returns for you. You've got work to do. And He wants to use you to accomplish His good plan on the earth. So let me recap and encourage you for a moment as I prepare to close out this timely message to you.

HE HAS COMMISSIONED YOU

As an IDENTIFIED woman in Christ, He has commissioned you to spread the Good News wherever you are and wherever He sends you. God wants to use *you* in these last days. I don't know if you can sense it, but time is winding down. Christ will return. But before He does, He is requiring us to share the gospel message with a dying, hurting, and lost world. Will you join this spiritual movement and tell others about Jesus? Will you stand up in the face of adversity for your faith and proclaim the gospel of Jesus Christ at all costs? The Holy Spirit will help you as you partner with Him to populate the Kingdom of Heaven. God will enable you. Look to His word in 2 Corinthians 1:21–22, "It is God who enables us, along with you, to stand firm for Christ. He has commissioned us, and he has identified us as his own by placing the Holy Spirit in our hearts as the first installment that guarantees everything he has promised us." He has commissioned you to help fulfill the Great Commission with the power that has been given unto you.

DON'T LOSE SIGHT OF YOUR IDENTITY

This is not the time to begin losing sight of who you are as a woman in Christ. You are who God says you are. Once you have accepted Christ, you are a child of God. You have been adopted into the faith and the Holy Spirit lives inside of you. Ephesians 1:13 says, "And when you believed in Christ, he identified you as his own by giving you the Holy Spirit, whom he promised long ago." So don't let anyone or anything change who God created you to be. Too many people, including those who proclaim to be a part of the body of Christ, are beginning to lose sight of who they are. Don't do that! Instead, grow in Christ and become who God called you to be on this earth. Be the woman He created you to be from your mother's womb and be who He called you to be through your purpose. So when someone asks, "Who are you?" Boldly proclaim, "I *am* IDENTIFIED. I *am* a child of God. I *am* who God called me to be." And there should be no doubt in anyone's mind that you are who you say you are, because you truly identify with Christ according to God's holy word. The world needs Jesus. And they need to see Him operating through you. So know your spiritual DNA and make your thumbprint in this world for Jesus Christ! Don't lose sight of your identity.

FLOW IN YOUR GOD-GIVEN GIFTS AND TALENTS

Remember, there is only one you! God made you unique and special. And He wants to use you to turn this world upside down for Christ! So once He shows you what He's placed inside of you, use your gifts and talents, and don't forget to cultivate them. And use them for God's glory and not the world. Follow Jesus all the way, and don't compromise for the fame of this world. Your gifts were given to you to bring glory and honor to God and to spread His Good News. Jesus tells us so in Mark 8:34–37, "Then, calling the crowd to join his disciples, he said, 'If any of you wants to be my follower, you must give up your own way, take up your cross, and follow me. If you try to hang on to your life, you will lose it. But if you give up your life for my sake and for the sake of the Good News, you will save it. And what do you benefit if you gain the whole world but lose your own soul? Is anything worth more than your soul?'"

We talked about the ten servants in the beginning, and the need for you to use well what God has given you. It's time-out for selfish ambition. If you sing, sing for Jesus. If you act, get in a casting call line for Christian films. If you write, write books, blogs, or film scripts that will minister to your audience, no self-help stuff. If you create things, create them to glorify God. The point here is this—as an IDENTIFIED woman in Christ, use your God-given gifts and talents to flow and operate for the Kingdom. It's time for Kingdom business! That's what *occupy* means. It means to engage the attention or energies, and to *do* business. Again, the world needs Jesus and the body of Christ needs to be built up. So whether you use your gifts in the local church, your community, job, or wherever God calls you…flow in them now. Put a HUGE smile on God's face and use what He has given you for His glory.

PREPARING YOURSELF PERSONALLY

As you prepare to move forward in your purpose, or even if you're already operating in it, personal preparation like consistent discipleship and discipline will be vital for your endurance and spiritual growth. You need to make sure that you're grounded in the word of God and in constant connection with the Lord through prayer, and even fasting when the Holy Spirit quickens you to do so. And don't forget about fellowship (this is one that I truly *love*)! Anyway, I talked about discipleship and personal discipline in detail in Chapter Three, so double back when you get a minute and grab those helpful nuggets. Spiritual nourishment through these crucial principles will be your additional sustenance as you walk out your purpose. And while you're staying rooted in the word, prayer, and fellowship, also keep a good handle on your work schedule. These suggestions will help you not only be strengthened yourself, but also prepare you to be ready to pour out to others when God quickens you.

IDENTIFIED THROUGH GODLY CHARACTER

This is a *big* one! I had to learn this one as I first felt the calling to minister to women thirteen years ago. Remember, our character will identify us. I discovered that it's one thing to have the knowledge and experience, but it's another thing to have *godly character*. And you and I know the weak spots. We all have flaws. But there is no excuse. Once we know, that's when we have to face the sheer reality that we need help. That's when we need to humbly go to God and say, "Lord, help me represent you well! Please fix my character." And guess what? He's faithful enough to do it through the power of His Holy Spirit (see Galatians 5:22–23). I would venture to say that nobody likes being around a crabby, mean, unloving, or prideful Christian. If you recall, the Bible gives us a glimpse of how important it is to have the right character *before* we move forward in our purpose. Psalm 105:19 shows us, "Until the time came to fulfill his dreams, the LORD tested Joseph's character." And most of us know the story of Joseph. I talked about it in an earlier chapter. But moving forward, biblical character is really HUGE when it comes down to fulfilling your purpose. Because God wants to make sure that you're ready for the outside world…that you're fully equipped for that big thing that you've been waiting on (if that's you). No matter who you are, your character, as a Christian woman, needs to match your representation. You're representing the King of Kings and Lord of Lords when you say you identify with Christ. The world doesn't need any more hypocrisy, arrogance, foolishness, or judgment from the people of God. They need Jesus. And they need to see Him operating in our callings through godly, biblical, and Holy Spirit-guided character. True proven godly character will help influence countless souls for the Kingdom of Heaven. So let's prove to the world that we do have love, joy, peace, patience, and gentleness while also showing forth God's goodness and faithfulness. And let's not forget about being humble, practicing self-control, having integrity and being forgiving. This is the evidence that proves that we are IDENTIFIED women!

COURAGEOUS WOMAN

I'm speaking life over you right now through these words, because you are a courageous woman! As you begin to advance in your purpose, God will give you the courage that you need to fulfill your calling. He did it with many of those whom He called throughout the Bible. Remember He told Joshua, "Be strong and courageous! Do not be afraid or discouraged. For the LORD your God will be with you wherever you go" (Joshua 1:9). Courage is all about stepping forward in faith. It's trusting God in the face of your fears. It's what I call, "Bold faith!" Courage is born through fearful times. Without a doubt, there are times when fearful things happen in our lives, but that's when God wants us to face them with faith. The devil would love to paralyze us here. But when those fearful moments happen in the natural sense, or when it comes down to moving forward in our purpose, that's when we have to make a conscious choice to take a firm grip and speak this very verse over ourselves. You have to tell yourself, "God doesn't want me to be fearful. He's calling me to be courageous. He will be with me wherever I go." Declare it and believe it. Another thing is, don't doubt God's ability in you. When God calls you to do something, He will be right there to help you with His victorious right hand. So don't doubt, don't waver, and don't question what only He can do. And please don't compare yourself to others as you do what God has called you to do. Be that strong and courageous woman, and keep moving forward. And I don't mean in a cocky or arrogant way. Stay humble. But go forth in what the Lord has predestined *you* to do. Because if you get hung up in fear, you will start fumbling on your end. Don't do it to yourself. Another thing, don't covet what your neighbor has, or what someone else is doing around you or in your field. That's a commandment! Instead, be excited about what God is doing through others and press on enthusiastically in what He's doing or going to do through you. Amen! It's time to let go of the fear, insecurity, doubt, and comparison game, and move forward courageously!

WINNING IN SPIRITUAL WARFARE

One thing about spiritual warfare is that you need to *expect it*. If you're going to do anything awesome for the Lord, expect an attack from our great enemy Satan. He is absolutely *not* excited about what God is doing or wants to do in your life. But remember, that's totally okay. You will just have to get some tough skin and put on the full armor of God and win!

Ephesians 6:11 says, "Put on all of God's armor, so that you will be able to stand firm against all strategies of the devil." There you have it! He will indeed throw fiery darts of fear, shame, guilt, condemnation, inferiority, and sometimes just plain foolishness at you to distract you from the task at hand. He'll even use people to try to get you to lose focus, but march on! Keep your eyes on Jesus, who is the author and finisher of your faith, while also keeping in mind that you are *not* wrestling against flesh and blood, but against principalities and spiritual wickedness in high places as Ephesians 6:12 declares. All of that is just the devil working up his schemes. Instead, submit yourself to God and do what James 4:7 states,

"Resist the enemy and he will flee from you." That is God's word, and it has fighting power! Don't ever forget, God's got your back and He will be with you in your battles.

Another thing that I want to encourage you with is this, when tests and trials come at you out of nowhere as you walk in your purpose, know that God is working things out behind the scenes. And even though some things may be really hard at times, just remember that your hard times now will be someone else's strength and comfort later. The Bible reassures of this in 2 Corinthians 1:3–4, "All praise to God, the Father of our Lord Jesus Christ. God is our merciful Father and the source of all comfort. He comforts us in all our troubles so that we can comfort others. When they are troubled, we will be able to give them the same comfort God has given us." So when the fight gets tough, hang in there, because God has a bigger plan. And recognize that you *may* be going through a trial, but also be open to the possibility that you just might be experiencing plain old *spiritual warfare*. No matter what it is, stand up, be strong, fight, and win!

BE EMPOWERED BY THE HOLY SPIRIT

The Holy Spirit will empower you to do great things in these last days. You just have to allow Him to be unleashed! Don't hold back the power. Instead, let the Holy Spirit move in your life, your church, and your community as He wants to move. Don't try to control Him, quench Him, forbid Him, or reject Him. He is your guide to all truth, your conviction when you need personal change, your boldness to proclaim the gospel message, and the power that is within you to do what God has commissioned you to do. So let Him have free course in your life. When you open your mouth to minister a word to someone in due season, let Him speak through you. When you sing, let Him sing through you. If you dance, let Him dance through you. If you pray, let Him pray through and for you. The Bible says in Ephesians 6:18, "Pray in the Spirit at all times and on every occasion. Stay alert and be persistent in your prayers for all believers everywhere." So don't neglect or hinder the power of the Holy Spirit. The Bible says in Acts 1:8, "But you will receive power when the Holy Spirit comes upon you. And you will be my witnesses, telling people about me everywhere—in Jerusalem, throughout Judea, in Samaria, and to the ends of the earth." Be a witness and be empowered by the Holy Spirit.

WHY THIS MESSAGE NOW?

Why is this message so important right now? Why is there such an urgency for the gospel to be preached? Why is there a great cry for revival and a spiritual awakening? Why do you need to be confident in who you are in Christ and begin moving forward in your purpose? Because the signs of Christ's return are becoming more and more evident. The birth pains described in Matthew 24:8 are getting stronger and stronger. But guess what?

Jesus tells us that before He returns, the gospel must be preached all over the world. In Matthew 24:14 He says, "And the Good News about the Kingdom will be preached throughout the whole world, so that all nations will hear it; and then the end will come." That's why this message is so important, sis. If you're reading this book right now, it's because God is giving us more time to fulfill the Great Commission before He sends His Son. This prophecy will be fulfilled.

God is simply giving more time so that people can come to know Him, but also for repentance. Let me remind you about what the Bible tells us in 2 Peter 3:9-10, "The Lord isn't really being slow about his promise, as some people think. No, he is being patient for your sake. He does not want anyone to be destroyed, but wants everyone to repent." Now here's the warning in verse 11, "But the day of the Lord will come as unexpectedly as a thief." It will be unexpected, swift, and visible. In Matthew 24:27 He continues, "For as the lightning flashes in the east and shines in the west, so it will when the Son of Man comes." (NLT)

Jesus tells us in Revelation 22:2, "And, behold, I come quickly; and my reward is with me, to give every man according as his work shall be. I am Alpha and Omega, the beginning and the end, the first, and the last." (KJV) Again, He is coming soon and it will be quick. I'm reminded of the parable of the ten bridesmaids in Matthew 25. Jesus tells His disciples a story about five bridesmaids who were wise and ready to meet the bridegroom (Jesus), and five bridesmaids who were foolish and *not* ready.

In this story He tells us in Matthew 25:10–11, "Then those who were ready went in with him to the marriage feast (heaven), and the door was locked. Later, when the other five bridesmaids returned, they stood outside, calling, 'Lord! Lord! Open the door for us!' But he called back, 'Believe me, I don't know you!'" They did not have the oil of the Holy Spirit within them! They waited too long to accept Him. They had not repented. They were not ready. So when He came, the door was locked shut. He did not know them. He could not identify them.

That's why this message is so vital and must be told now. That's why we have a major role to play in these last days. That's why we are on this evangelistic mission. The Good News about the soon coming King and Kingdom must be preached—*but we must also keep watch*. Jesus tells us in Matthew 24:42–44, "So you, too, must keep watch! For you don't know what day your Lord is coming. Understand this: If a homeowner knew exactly when a burglar was coming, he would keep watch and not permit his house to be broken into. You also must be ready all the time, for the Son of Man will come when least expected."

Jesus *is* coming back, and when He does there won't be time for any excuses. We just witnessed this through Scripture. I don't know about you, but this puts a fresh charge in me to help others accept Jesus Christ and get the oil of the Holy Spirit before it's too late! But it also helps me to keep watch! Sis, once we are IDENTIFIED and living for the King of Kings and Lord of Lords, then we can have the power to help others to be IDENTIFIED, too.

With all of this that being said, you need to also know that as we fulfill this Great Commission, we will face opposition, resistance, and persecution. As Christians, we will have to endure some hard times and tribulations in this life. Jesus already forewarned us of these things ahead of time. He said in John 15:20, "Do you remember what I told you? A slave is not greater than the master. Since they persecuted me, naturally they will persecute you." He also said in John 16:1 and 33, "I have told you these things so that you won't abandon your faith—These things I have spoken unto you, that in me ye might have peace. In the world ye shall have tribulation: but be of good cheer, I have overcome the world."

Jesus often had pretty deep conversations with His disciples. One night they asked Jesus privately about the end times. They asked, "Tell us, when will all this happen? What sign will signal your return and the end of the world" (Matthew 24:3, NLT)? And Jesus went on to explain various events that would occur that would lead up to His return. Then He told them, "Immediately after the tribulation of those days shall the sun be darkened, and the moon shall not give her light, and the stars be shaken: And then shall appear the Son of man coming in the clouds of heaven with power and great glory. And he shall send his angels with a great sound of a trumpet, and they shall gather together his elect from the four winds, from one end of heaven to the other." (KJV)

That's what Jesus told them. This passage of Scripture is referencing the sign of His return. Many Christians call the return of Christ, the Rapture and/or Judgment. But when you have some free time, I highly recommend that you read all of Matthew

24, 1 Thessalonians 4:15-18, and 2 Thessalonians 2) for further understanding of these times that Jesus is talking about.

In the meantime, as we wait for that glorious day of His return, it's important to note what Jesus said in Mark 13:32-33, "However, no one knows the day or hour when these things will happen, not even the angels in heaven or the Son himself. Only the Father knows. And since you don't know when that time will come, be on guard! Stay alert!" (NLT)

It's wise to be a woman who is alert, and discerns the times with *great expectancy*. Titus 2:11-15 says, "For the grace of God has been revealed, bringing salvation to all people. And we are instructed to turn from godless living and sinful pleasures. We should live in this evil world with wisdom, righteousness, and devotion to God, while we look forward with hope to that wonderful day when the glory of our great God and Savior, Jesus Christ, will be revealed. He gave his life to free us from every kind of sin, to cleanse us, and to make us his very own people, totally committed to doing good deeds." (NLT)

I echo the words of Paul which says, "And so, dear friends, while you are waiting for these things to happen, make every effort to be found living peaceful lives that are pure and blameless in his sight. And remember, our Lord's patience gives people time to be saved."

IT'S TIME TO PREPARE YE THE WAY OF THE LORD

There you have it! Jesus is coming back, but He's giving more time for us to help build the Kingdom! It's time to occupy until Jesus returns. It's time to be a modern day John the Baptist! We have got to cry loud!

I actually love John's wild and unapologetic boldness. He was totally unashamed of the message He was proclaiming! He knew what he was called to do and he did it. He didn't care what he looked like, or what people thought about him as he shouted loudly, "Prepare, ye the way of the Lord," (Mark 1:3 KJ21).

John the Baptist was preparing people for the first coming of Christ, but we are called to prepare people for His return. Do you see the state of the world, not to mention the state of the global church? Jesus is still calling for repentance from the inside out. When Jesus started His ministry the Bible tells us in Matthew 4:17, "From then on Jesus began to preach, 'Repent of your sins and turn to God, for the Kingdom of Heaven is near.'" The Kingdom of Heaven is at hand.

The church needs revival, and the world is in need of a spiritual awakening. We all need to have repentant hearts. And as it relates to the church (us), we need to make sure that we are hot and on fire for the Lord—not lukewarm right now (see Revelations 3:16). I believe God is on the move! The only question now is, are we going to join the movement?

It's not about us, sis. It's not what we look like and it's not about what people will think of us if we begin radically and boldly proclaiming the gospel message of Jesus Christ to the lost. They need a Savior and they need a purified, wise bride. It's time for us, as the church, to wake up. It's time for us to arise from the comfortable slumber.

We need to see a mighty move of God's power sweeping over our nation and this world like the book of Acts. We need to see thousands experiencing salvation again! Jesus said that we would do even greater and mightier things than He did. So what is the church waiting for? What are you waiting for, sis?

I am praying for the laborers right now, for this end time harvest. Jesus needs more laborers in the field. He said in Luke 10:2–3, "The harvest is great, but the workers are few. So pray to the Lord who is in charge of the harvest; ask Him to send more workers into His fields." Will you join me in prayer, so we can move forward in our purpose and turn this world upside down for Jesus? Will you rise up to the plate and take your place in your local church, your community, your city, your social media networks—our world?

It's time for the laborers to rise up, take our places all over this globe, and prepare ye the way of the Lord! It's time to help win the lost to Christ. It doesn't matter who they are. It doesn't matter if they are prostitutes, psychics, the occult, gay, lesbians, demon-possessed, devil worshipers, murderers, adulterers, fornicators, criminals, or the rich. From the least to the greatest, it's time for the body of Christ (the church) to rise up to help the captives be set free, be changed, healed, and delivered in the mighty name of Jesus Christ and with the power of the Holy Spirit!

It's time to be bold and stand strong in the faith no matter what happens. So don't be shaken and don't be hindered! Instead, maintain your identity in Christ and be steadfast in your faith. This gospel message *must* be preached. And I believe as we stand together as one in Christ and in love, we will see a time of great harvest of souls in this end time generation!

It's time to unleash the power that is within you and make your thumbprint in the world for Jesus Christ! It's time to prepare ye the way of the Lord! Join this spiritual movement across the globe and occupy until He comes. It's time to know who you are in Christ, grow in your faith, move forward in your purpose, and show the world that you are **IDENTIFIED** and *they* can be too!

READ MORE & STAY CONNECTED TO INSIDE OUT WITH COURTNAYE

Printed in the United States
By Bookmasters